Paying Attention

Advance Praise for
Paying Attention

"'Attention is the origin of faith, hope, and love,' according to Nicephorus the Solitary, a fourteenth-century monk of Mt. Athos, and many Christian writers agree: the way we attend or fail to attend to God and neighbor is a real measure of our spiritual life. Now Gary Peluso-Verdend applies this principle to the life of congregations, offering a practical, hopeful, lucid, and graceful guide to the flourishing of congregations in an epoch of ever-increasing distraction."

—Carol Zaleski
Smith College

"In *Paying Attention*, Gary Peluso-Verdend offers readers a new and fresh look into congregations as places where attention is taught and focused on Jesus. In a world of lumpy theological pabulum, the good professor serves up a hearty stew. He throws in meaty batches of imaginative and thoughtful ingredients— congregational conflict, church growth, ecclesiology, theology, leadership. His writing invites readers into their own 'what-if's, and his propositions are intriguing. Because attention remains the world's most valuable commodity, *Paying Attention* can give new understanding—and new hope—to congregational leaders."

—Bob Sitze
author of *Your Brain Goes to Church: Neurobiology and Congregational Life*

"Gary Peluso-Verdend gives congregations a roadmap on how to cultivate attentiveness—like that of Jesus—for rediscovering their vocation. Employing both biblical and classical texts of spiritual formation, *Paying Attention* develops a snapshot of what an attentive church filled with self-knowledge and confidence in its gifts looks like. Peluso-Verdend's astute analysis of contemporary mainline congregational life and new model of leadership teams will prove an invaluable companion in your church's journey toward purposeful, attentive faithfulness."

—Kay Bessler Northcutt
Phillips Theological Seminary

"*Paying Attention* compellingly says that being prayerfully and mindfully attentive to the things of God lies at the heart of being church. Peluso-Verdend offers helpful ways of being attentive to God and God's people as the way of deepening personal and congregational faith and effectiveness. This is much-needed advice in a world filled with books on 40 days to a better church, programs in a box, and easy steps to Christian community. *Paying Attention* leads us into the deep places of the soul—the places where congregations pay attention to the unique mission to which God has called them."

—J. Brent Bill
author of *Holy Silence: The Gift of Quaker Spirituality*

Paying Attention

Focusing Your Congregation on What Matters

Gary E. Peluso-Verdend

THE
ALBAN
INSTITUTE

Herndon, Virginia
www.alban.org

The Alban Institute
2121 Cooperative Way, Suite 100
Herndon, VA 20171-5370

Scripture quotations, unless otherwise noted, are from the New Revised Standard Version of the Bible, copyright © 1989, Division of Christian Education of the National Council of the Churches of Christ in the United States of America and are used by permission.

Cover design by Adele Robey, Phoenix Graphics.

Library of Congress Cataloging-in-Publication Data

Peluso-Verdend, Gary E.
  Paying attention : focusing your congregation on what matters / Gary E. Peluso-Verdend.
     p. cm.
  Includes bibliographical references.
  ISBN 1-56699-308-3
  1. Attention—Religious aspects—Christianity. 2. Mission of the church. I. Title.

BV640.P45 2005
254—dc22
                          2005011471

  10   09   08   07   06   05   VG   1   2   3   4   5   6

Contents

Foreword

There is a sweatshirt you can buy these days with a catchy phrase emblazoned on the front: *"They say I have ADD, but they just don't understand. Oh look! A chicken!"* It's a piece of apparel that ought to sell well in America. ADD (Attention Deficit Disorder) is now a household term that everybody seems to know something about. Psychiatric scientists aren't entirely sure whether there is a steep rise in actual cases of persons living with some form of attention deficit disorder, or whether there is simply more awareness of its consequences and thus more hasty diagnoses occurring. Whatever the case, most people have some sense of the crippling symptoms of this disorder. They have seen it in friends. At times, they may have even feared its onset in their own lives.

We're well versed in plotting how an individual human mind easily gets distracted. We're experts at analyzing how the misfiring of brain neurons can contribute to a person's lack of focus. But rarely do we talk about institutions being afflicted with attention deficit disorder. It simply isn't in our vocabulary. We're not trained to think of "developing the practice of paying attention" as a key responsibility for an organization.

Take churches as an example. Effective congregations all over the map plan wisely for the reshaping and refining of their mission. It's a constant project they undertake, though one that usually gets special attention at a targeted time each year. Leaders in these churches convene for an annual retreat or a special set of meetings and take stock of where their congregation is strong, weak, or full of unrealized potential. Some parishes call these key meetings strategic planning opportunities. Others think of them as important vision moments. Whatever they are called in your congregation, chances are good that every asset, resource, and blessing in your midst gets discussed, except for one—PAYING ATTENTION.

Congregations are notoriously guilty of spending energy on creating and sustaining new programs at the expense of doing the key central tasks of their mission extremely well. Gary Peluso-Verdend calls the task of paying attention "the most precious gift in a congregation's life." He is determined to get congregations less obsessed with novelty as their chief goal and efficiency as their governing principle and more finely tuned to delivering meaning and purpose that celebrates God in their midst.

Peluso-Verdend believes that focusing on those areas of ministry that bring us closer to God is where our primary ecclesiastical attention is due. In most congregations, he argues, this is a matter of filtering out less important things in order for the worship of the Lord (and the hospitality amongst the Lord's people) to have our undivided attention.

The desire to pay closer attention to the activity of God, and not to our own busyness, is as old as the Hebrew people. There is a moment in the life of Moses that gave historic shape to this long struggle of the church battling its self-focused tendencies. The story from Exodus goes like this: Moses is tending his father-in-law's sheep one day. He knew those sheep of Jethro well. They had his sustained attention, we might say, at least until one particular day when Moses turned his head. Sometime between breakfast and dinner that day, as theologian and historian Patrick Henry retells the story, Moses turned his head. It would prove to be a turning point in history. By nightfall he would no longer be whistling at sheep. He would be responsible for liberating a whole nation from slavery.

Jewish legend has it that God had to do something extraordinary to get Moses' attention from those sheep. What would this be? God would startle Moses with a burning bush. "I must turn aside and look at this great sight, and see why the bush is not burned up," says Moses (Exod. 3:3). God is after Moses' attention, and God gets it. Scripture tells us that Moses turns and looks. The rest is history. We never again hear what happens to those sheep of Jethro. We do know the compelling presence of God is powerful enough to unbuckle the sandals on Moses' feet. He finds himself standing barefoot on holy ground.

If our churches are overly self-focused, or ADD-stricken in any sense of the word, the people within them are going to struggle to know when they are ever standing on holy ground. How will we know when to turn our heads for Godly things, if our heads are always buried in things we thought we had to do? If our congregations are operating in near-constant fear of missing something better, scanning the world for the latest fads, how will they ever attend meaningfully to the steady mercies of God? If multitasking continues to evolve as that virtue of highest reward, how will we avoid the mess of an unfocused life? These are some of the questions to which Gary Peluso-Verdend wants congregations to give greater attention.

The author highlights key focal practices that wise congregations will devote energy to. Shaped as we are by that which captures our first attention, Peluso-Verdend reasons that it is in the best interest of our congregations to think beyond what simply generates high activity. Vitality will come to the pews of those churches that are prepared to "keep the main thing the main thing."

Paying Attention: Focusing Your Congregation on What Matters is not a book that will go down well for readers addicted to continuous partial attention. But for those willing to take on the chapters ahead, here's a suggestion before reading: unplug the iPod, turn off the e-mail, silence the cell phone, keep the mail out of view, and wait on setting the microwave for your Turkey Tetrazzini. Only then will you be able to concentrate on what your congregation might do to turn its head differently and notice the awesome presence of God.

Peter W. Marty, senior pastor
St. Paul Lutheran Church, Davenport, Iowa
Host, Grace Matters Radio

Preface

Keeping focused while writing a book on attention has challenged me. By profession, I am a seminary administrator who also teaches. My everyday work includes a sometimes attention-scattering combination of e-mails, phone calls, appointments, lesson preparations, projects, and off-campus seminary-related commitments. Worthy goals and important issues compete for my energy and attention—as do less worthy endeavors. My seminary granted me a sabbatical that I peppered with regular-time commitments (and sometimes the "peppered" commitments overwhelmed the sabbatical time). At home, my wife and I live in an older house that has needed attention and, when we found the roof leak that wrecked a bathroom or the broken heat exchanger in the furnace, more than a little money. Expending house-related time, energy, attention, and money have all accelerated from the time we decided to move to a new position in a different state. Keeping up with my children's changing lives has also taken goodly attention. And, a year ago, when I was trying to make progress on this book, two relatively small incisions to remove a cancerous spot from my left shoulder, along with the nearby lymph nodes, caught my attention disproportionately to the size of the visible scars.

I knew from the outset a truth that has only grown more significant in the eighteen months or so of writing this book: I need to pay attention to how—and to what and whom—I pay attention, and to strengthen my ability to do so. Through sharing my developing thoughts with many clergy and laity, I confirmed that I am not alone in needing to live this truth. Many, many of us, including the institutions we care about and care through, struggle to attend rightly. We live in a powerfully distracting age. Attention is the most precious gift any person or institution can give. As Christians and as congregations, we should take care regarding when, where, and to whom to give it.

I am deeply thankful to Garrett-Evangelical Theological Seminary, President Ted Campbell, Dean Jack Seymour, and my faculty colleagues for granting me the semester-long sabbatical that provided the calendar space necessary to begin this project. A gathering of United Methodist conference council directors, several opportunities to speak with other United Methodist conference-level administrators, and adult classes and retreats at Wesley United Methodist Church, Urbana, Illinois, First United Methodist Church in Glen Ellyn, Illinois, and Evergreen Christian Church in Evergreen, Colorado all helped me to develop and test the connections between the personal and institutional resources of attention, time, energy, and money.

While writing, I have reflected on the teachers who most helped me to focus my vision and frame the world: my parents, Dolly and Emil Peluso; my youth counselor, the late Ben Sattem; my high school German teacher and wise friend, the late Wilfried Wilke; my academic mentor and college New Testament professor, Lamar Cope; and my high school friend's father who later served as my dissertation advisor, a scholar-pastor whom I have admired and respected for over thirty years now, Martin Marty.

I am grateful to my wife, Cheri Peluso-Verdend, who has encouraged me in this project every step of the way. I am also indebted to David Lott, editor, who strengthened this book tremendously through a deft combination of critical questions, wise decisions regarding where to expand and what to cut, believing in the topic's importance, and timely encouraging words. Any deficits or errors remain my own.

Gary E. Peluso-Verdend
Holy Week, 2005

Introduction

A Martha-Minded Church

*Attention—Your Congregation's
Most Precious Gift*

The evangelist in Luke 10:38–42 tells the story of Martha and Mary, two sisters who receive Jesus as a guest. Luke tells us that Martha busies herself with many tasks, probably the tasks of preparing space and food for him. Certainly, these are acts of hospitality. Mary, in the meantime, sits at Jesus' feet and listens. Perhaps Martha wants to be there, too, but she has all these tasks. Indirectly, Martha rebukes her sister by asking Jesus to break off talking with her and insisting that Mary help her with the hospitality. What Martha asks is consistent with women's conventional roles in her world. The Gospel's first audiences most likely would have sided with Martha. Make her sister work! But, as Jesus does so often (and as we shall explore in chapter 3), he rejects conventional mores. He tells Martha that she is anxious and distracted by many things—perhaps even worthy things. Our translations of Jesus' "diagnosis" of Martha's mental state do not express the drama in his words. At their roots, one word means "to divide" (*merimnas*) and the other "to be in an uproar" (*thorubase*). Martha's attention is divided. She scatters a most precious gift and, to borrow a phrase from another religion, her scattered mind expresses itself like a screaming monkey. Jesus reframes for Martha what is timely and important, which is what Mary is doing.[1]

And what is Mary doing? Commentators claim that she is listening to his teaching, being discipled. Certainly. But I would also claim that she is giving Jesus the gift of her undivided presence. She gives Jesus her attention.

Many old mainline congregations[2] today offer Jesus a Martha-minded, attention-divided people, assailed by a cacophony of voices telling us what to do, framing for us what the pressing goods are, visioning for us what our future is, and fostering fear in those who do not heed the saving advice. Furthermore, because we are shaped by what we attend to (see chapter 2) and how we frame our questions, divided and dissipated attention is not only a problem in and of itself. Attention also steers how we use our resources of time, energy, and money. Dissipated attention leads to poor stewardship of resources. When we squander our attention, we also waste the resources God has given us to fulfill the mission to which we are called.

I believe it is a very good time for the church to strengthen the practices of giving Jesus our best attention. I write this book in hopes of persuading you that this is the case and of offering some practical suggestions regarding how we can develop the practices of paying Jesus attention.

Disposed to Distraction—Perfected

Why is it hard to give Jesus our undivided, quiet attention? In order to develop more of a Mary-minded church, we need to know what is distracting us and why—what meaning the distractions hold in our lives. On the one hand, the answer may be so obvious that the question seems silly. *Where, in our society, do we give anyone or anything our quiet, undivided attention for any sustained, meaningful period of time?* Jesus is in the same boat with the others in our lives—he gets pieces of us. We have even fashioned divided attention into a virtue and named it "multitasking." One sees this "virtue" listed as a desired competency in job ads. Our society rewards those who act as if they can always take on one more thing.

On the other hand, if one reads the writings of Christian hermits from the early centuries, we find that it has always been hard for Christians to give Jesus our best attention, to do the one needful thing, to lay down our obsessions and anxieties in order to receive Christ's gift of his presence, his kingdom, here and now. For example, the hermits featured in the *Philokalia* reflect extensively on the human capacity to be distracted, especially by the thoughts, images, and feelings our minds generate. We human beings do not need cell phones, computers, TVs, movies, and oodles of other gadgets and screens to be distracted. Given the brain's disposition to notice novelty and to lead us to seek pleasure and avoid pain, we can be distracted perfectly well in solitude.

But the combination of our human disposition to give our attention in bytes and our contemporary culture that provides a legion of opportunities to perfect that disposition has taken its toll on congregations. *I am suggesting that we look at the plight of very busy congregations as organizations that participate in a form of institutional attention deficit disorder.*

Now, I do not have empirical, quantified evidence to back this claim that that many congregations are distracted. I have not done a survey or conducted hundreds of focus groups. But the anecdotal evidence is deep, both in writers on local church life as well as in conversations among church folks. I invite you to consider the question: *does the congregation you know best demonstrate a kind of institutional attention deficit disorder?*

Brain researcher Dr. John Ratey wrote this about attention deficit hyperactive disorder in individuals:

> ADHD can be thought of as an addiction to the present. Patients are often quick to act because they are hooked on immediate feedback. They tend to prioritize tasks according to which offers the most immediate gratification. As a result, they tend to not interrupt current activities in order to rehearse skills or evaluate the consequences of their actions.[3]

Addicted to the present. Hooked on immediate feedback. Avoid the difficult in favor of immediate gratification. Acting without rehearsing skills or evaluating consequences. Accenture consultants and authors Thomas Davenport and John Beck claim most of this is true for American businesses. University classics professor Stephen Bertman decries "addiction to the now" as one of the diseases of a society moving faster than it is humanly healthy to do.[4]

It is important to understand that the phrases "addicted to the present" or to "the now" do not imply presence. Both Ratey and Bertman use the word *addicted*, acting now without purpose other than to persist in tapping whatever is giving pleasure in the moment. Do not picture the mindful monk or nun in deep prayer in the presence of Christ. Rather, conjure the image of a teenager with music blaring, a TV on for background noise, instant-messaging a friend while playing an online video game—and homework is waiting.

Congregations tend to behave in a manner consistent with the pace of life and frames of meaning that their members bring from the larger society. It stands to reason, then, that a society that mindlessly fosters attention deficiencies will contribute toward distracted congregations. You may want to question or argue about one or more of the descriptors I offered above. But I ask you to consider whether all of these are strands of a single braid: our inability to sustain attention on the same end long enough—and the discipline to dedicate sufficient resources of time, energy, and money—to see real change in a positive direction. I have worked with pastors, with judicatory officials, with seminary faculty and administrators, and with ecumenical- and interfaith-agency leaders for over a decade. Each group complains about sustaining the attention of their constituencies—and of their employed staffs—long enough to see change or even to evaluate whether or not they did what they set out to do.

The Attraction of Distractions

Why are we so distractable? Brain researchers tell us that human beings are wired to seek pleasure, to avoid pain, and to notice novelty. Recent brain research findings describe what is called *neuroplasticity*: throughout our lives, the connections and pathways in our brains are shaped and reshaped by what we do and by what happens to us. The paths and connections between brain cells change as we learn or, less consciously, as we are entertained and amused while we sit in front of screens: TV, LCD, video games, and the like. Plato worried about what kind of music people listened to because he believed that music shaped character. Ancient teachers admonished that we become what we look at (as in "the eye is the lamp of the body" [Matt. 6:22]). Brain research demonstrates that our brains are, indeed, shaped by what we attend to, by what we take in through our senses, consciously or not.

Through our participation in our technology-driven society, we are wiring ourselves to maximize our potentials to embrace novelty, to avoid pain, and to seek pleasure. Our love for the new is so pervasive and well known that it is hardly necessary to offer examples. One could interpret our use of drugs, alcohol, ear-blasting music, sex, putting more hours per year into the wage economy than any other advanced society, Starbucks fixes, health-club memberships, and many other "treats" we give ourselves as efforts to dull or avoid pain and increase pleasure.[5] Our society offers more opportunities to be distracted than any other in history. Our affluence, the relative reliability of food resources, our technology, our consumer mind-set, and our love of "progress" all contribute.

Consider the distractions an automobile driver in an urban area such as Chicago might be contending with while moving along (at good times of the day) at sixty-five miles an hour (which, by the way, is over the speed limit but keeps one from being mowed down by the majority of drivers who are in even a bigger hurry!):

- Billboards with catchy slogans, seductive graphics, and up-to-the-minute mortgage rates

- Cell phone calls—making them, receiving them (hopefully not playing with the video game and text messaging functions, or receiving visuals of who-knows-what)[6]
- Construction congestion and lane changes
- Weather
- Changing the radio station, the CD, or the tape
- Lots and lots of crazed or crazy, hurried, distracted drivers

Distractions in contemporary life are legion. Tort laws contain a concept called "attractive nuisance." If a homeowner builds a beautiful backyard in-ground pool, visible to all the surrounding neighbors and beyond, yet fails to erect a fence to protect temptable children and teens from entering the pool, the homeowner is liable for damages because she or he produced an attractive nuisance. In twenty-first-century United States society, we have become expert at constructing attractive nuisances that attract our attention, sap our energies, use up our time, and on which we spend billions of dollars.

Critics of our contemporary culture shoot at our screens. Both TV and the Internet swamp us with data. The late Neil Postman asserted that we are amusing ourselves to death, drowning in data, and that we could use some reliable institutional filters to help us determine which data is worthy information. Mihaly Csikszentmihalyi claims that passive forms of entertainment, such as TV, leave us depressed and drain energy that should be devoted to complex activities that are much better suited to contribute to happiness. In *Bowling Alone*, Robert Putnam points to TV-watching as a key factor in the decrease of civic participation when one compares the World War II generation with those raised after TV sets became part of the culture.[7]

Of course, on one level, most of that to which I refer is not a distraction; it is a message seeking our attention. A great many of these "distractions" are, in fact, advertisements, messages for which someone paid good money to grab our attention. Attractive distractions exist to sell us products produced to light up the pleasure centers in our brains (more so with TV than the Internet, although the latter is rapidly becoming the most powerful commercial medium in the world). As Christians, we forget at our peril that television, commercially produced movies, and a great deal of the Web exist to sell, to feed the image of human beings as *homo consumericus*, that to be human is to consume. Consider the U.S. American calendar. Calendars exist to help us order time, to tell us what season it is, and what activity is timely for that season. Now, if we pay attention to a powerful American calendar—the shopping calendar—we might think that shopping gives meaning to life. Christmas, after-Christmas, New Year's, Super Bowl, President's Day, Valentine's Day, Easter, Mother's Day, Memorial Day sales, vacation, Fourth of July sales, Back-to-School sales, Labor Day sales, Columbus Day sales, Halloween, overlapping with Christmas, and Thanksgiving wedged in—behold, the American calendar in which we are encouraged through every TV, print, Internet, and movie commercial to live and move and have our being.

Distractions and Avoidance

Our society's legion of attractive distractions not only light up our pleasure centers and tempt us with more novelty than we can ever attend to. Distractions also help us to avoid, especially to avoid pain. Sometimes we seek distractions to occupy our attention and keep us from being present to the people and circumstances around us. If being present would mean dealing with pain—one's own or that of one's community or world—then distractions can keep that pain at arm's length, at least.

As I will argue below, the distracted behavior of congregations can be a form of pain avoidance. The church is a people called to a cruciform life—that is, a life shaped by Jesus, who attends to human sufferers with healing and hope. When we follow distractions rather than pick up our cross and follow Jesus, the church treks that wide path toward unfaithfulness.

Theologian Douglas John Hall believes that relatively affluent North American Christians are particularly susceptible to being distracted from our work of bearing "the cross in our context." Hall cites Martin Luther's distinction between a *theologia crucis* (theology of the cross, of suffering) and a *theologia gloriae* (a theology of triumph). The American faith in progress and "I'm getting better every day" dispose us toward a theology of glory. If we are to increase our capacity to be an attentive church, a cruciform church within our context, we will have to seek en-couragement (literally, strength in the heart) to increase our ability to be present with those who suffer—including with ourselves.

Obsession and Anxiety

Two categories of distraction are obsession and anxiety. Obsession and anxiety are two of the great vampires of attention.

The word *obsession* comes from a word meaning "besiege, occupy, possess."[8] To be obsessed means to be fixated on a past event, circumstance, or relationship with the hope of "fixing" it.[9] But the object can only be a fixation—it is glued to a place we cannot reach. When we are obsessed, our attention is besieged, occupied, possessed by something broken, past, and unfixable.

To be obsessed, in the way I am using the term here, means to be fixated on something *past*. Anxiety, ostensibly, concerns the *future*. The root of the word *anxious* means "to choke or be in distress."[10] A person or organization that is anxious is distressed about something that may be. Now, our concerns about what may be are highly conditioned by our obsessions and perceptions about what has been. Thus, seeing through anxious eyes, the pasts constrain us in the present, choking our options that could lead to a different future. When we are anxious, we misuse our freedom to act.

Obsession and anxiety are, largely, behaviors that waste and dissipate attention. These behaviors keep us from living in the only time we can ever control: now. The only time in which we make a decision about how to live is now. Obsessions and anxieties focus us on the unfixable past or the uncontrollable future. To live in the now, to be present to the persons and issues that God has entrusted to us, to use our freedom to take a purposeful step in the now toward a desired future, is very different from being *addicted* to the now, as ADD has been characterized. Living in the now is not anxiously or obsessing tapping our brain's pleasure center like a rat in a lab experiment might do.

Jesus of Nazareth's ability to be fully attentive and present to people was remarkable, as we shall see in chapter 3. I am convinced that his attentiveness was an essential element of his personal and interpersonal healing powers. To be fully attentive to another, to behold them, is the most precious gift any person can give another. Surely, sometimes the other needs drink, sometimes food, sometimes shelter or clothing or medical care. But we don't give those resources if we are not present and paying attention.

The Shape of This Book

Attention is also the most precious gift that the church can give. I hope this book will persuade you that Christians should pay attention to how we give our attention and to strengthen our ability to attend as Christ attends—not just in our personal, individual lives, but as a corporate body as well.

In the first chapter, I will turn attention to four concerns that claim substantial resources from congregations today: increasing size; preservation; utilizing technology; dealing with symptomatic conflict. Each of these concerns embeds both legitimate and important commitments and potential for serious distraction and dissipated attention. In chapter 2, I will develop an understanding of what attention is and, specifically, of Christian attention as presence to God and neighbor. Chapter 3 will examine Jesus' teachings and ministry as they relate to attention. The fourth and fifth chapters will address Christian practices of attending and of strengthening attention. I will begin with the practice of theology, followed by a fictional conversation in a congregation among people trying to practice theology. Then, in chapter 5, I will develop potential relationships between other Christian practices and attention, before concluding with a chapter on leading an attentive congregation.

Each of the chapters will also include study questions. I wrote this book in hopes that leadership teams, comprised of lay and clergy, would read it together. The questions are either at the end of the chapter or interspersed within the chapter.

Chapter 1

Size, Preservation, Technology, Conflict

Four Attention Challenges for the Church

When I think about the strengths of a faithful and effective congregation, what comes to mind are a robust sense of its particular mission, a clear understanding of the living tradition that feeds its life, a faithful and compelling presentation of the gospel message for today, and the capacity to engage redemptively with suffering. I am certain that there are other very important strengths to consider. But these four stand out for me because I see attractive distractions, somewhat peculiar to our time, that limit a congregation's ability to attend to these strengths. Congregations are distracted (1) by arguments about size rather than mission; (2) by preservation of buildings and programs rather than the living tradition that is worthy of passing on; (3) by putting hope in technology rather than their understanding of the gospel; and (4) by spending themselves on symptoms of conflict rather than on major roots of suffering. I further believe that the way congregations play out these distracted behaviors expresses elements of obsession and of anxiety. I hope that by focusing attention on these four challenges congregational leaders will release energy and attention away from distracted behaviors and toward developing these critical strengths.

Challenge: Size and Mission

When I was a seminary student in the late 1970s, I recall professors criticizing church leaders who emphasized numerical growth. A prophetic church, they said, might be a smaller church, a "righteous remnant" of the once-bloated post–World War II church, full of cultural Christians held

1

captive by the value of market share. If I had ten dollars for each time we were told, "The church is called to be faithful, not effective"—well, I'd have more money! One can still find this critique in at least some seminary faculties. But a student is more likely to find faculty members speaking positively about evangelism, congregational renewal, and the like than a student might have heard twenty-five years ago. Today, we seminary faculty members are likely to advocate for both faithfulness and effectiveness. Numerical growth is not a value in and of itself; however, we do value healthy congregations and, in many cases, healthy congregations will grow numerically and spiritually.

A significant demographic shift has also fostered this attention to congregational size. A recent national congregations study demonstrates that the majority of Christians in the United States are worshiping in a relatively small percentage of congregations that average more than four hundred in worship weekly. But the great majority of congregations boast of less than seventy worshipers each week. In other words, middle-sized congregations are disappearing.[1]

National news magazines and other mass media bring their spotlights to the large congregations and to megachurches with more than a thousand weekly worshipers. In the meantime, small-membership churches—whether in rural areas, in transitional urban areas, or older suburban locations—disappear from the sights of all but their own members and struggle to afford educated leaders and program dollars.

Mainline Protestant congregations often represent that shrinking middle and those thousands of small-membership congregations founded before 1960. In business terms, this means that mainline Protestant congregations have lost market share. The rate of decline for some has slowed; the ratio of membership to worship attendance shows signs of improving. But the losses are real. Many, many congregations founded before 1960 are much smaller than they once were. At the same time, however, the mainline has increased the number of large and very large churches. Denominational officials are turning their attention to large congregations as teaching churches, as curriculum-resource developers, as research and development laboratories for ministry to younger generations, and as planters of new Christian communities.

This attention to large congregations is warranted, but it can go too far. It can tempt leaders of not-large churches to distraction. Every congregation is not called to be *large*. Every congregation is called to fulfill its particular *mission*, to be faithful and effective *given its distinctive mission*. I am concerned that leaders in not-large churches, and sometimes denominational leaders, either look to large churches for how to be church without questioning whether "one size fits all," or they decide that they do not fit the cultural trend toward bigness and, therefore, have no future. For such congregations, I want to place some limits on the value of size and hoist the flag on valuing mission.

Of course, there is practical value in knowing a congregation's size. One should lead a small-membership church much differently than a large-membership church. A smaller congregation enduring growth pains requires a different kind of attention to making a transition to multiple worship services than does the erstwhile middle-size congregation that can no longer afford to pay a choir director.

But, in congregational life, do we value bigness per se? If you belong to a congregation in which three thousand people worship on a weekend, what is your attitude toward the rural congregation with sixty in attendance, or the city congregation that feeds nine hundred souls a week in their soup kitchen (with a combination of government grants and mission giving from large-membership congregations such as your own) but whose average worship attendance has dipped below forty?

Similarly, what is the value of the language of "market share" as applied to our congregations? Why do we, through our congregations, need to increase market share? Some congregational leaders, after objecting to the business terminology, would argue that being faithful to "The Great Commission" (Matt. 28:18-20) will grow the church. Maybe. But there is also an affinity between the American evangelical and mainline conception of evangelism and American business: both tend to believe that institutions must expand or die. Fundamentally, both share the underlying plotline of a highly competitive environment with very scarce resources. Compete and grow numerically—or die.

I believe it is this simple plot or one-line narrative that drives congregations to obsessive and anxious behaviors. You may have heard the saying, "The church is always one generation away from extinction." This is true—unless the faith is passed on to and received by the following generation, the church, in a form akin to what we know now, could not survive. But the "compete and grow—or die" narrative actually limits thinking and options, especially theologically informed thinking, about the present mission of each congregation in its place.

When I lived in suburban Tulsa, a city with dozens of large congregations, I talked with the pastor of a congregation where over seven hundred people worshiped each Sunday. His board was constantly drawing comparisons between their congregation and the twenty thousand-plus-member congregation up the street, complete with indoor skating rink and Christmas light display featuring millions of lights—and finding themselves wanting. The board's anxiety may "lead" the congregation to devalue its gifts and to focus on "the need" to add more programs, hoping to increase market share and compete with "the big boys." I would call such congregations "ADD congregations." They think they must *add* one more thing, but that adding exceeds the capacity of their attention and dissipates the power of their resources, leading them further into being an attention-deficit-disordered (ADD!) congregation.

Leaders in middle-sized congregations fear becoming small and concern themselves about how to grow big—also an anxious reaction. Many, many small-membership congregations live in buildings that either whisper or scream, "You were once big." A congregation's reaction to this message may be either obsessive or anxious. The *obsession* often expresses itself in the desire to preserve, to maintain a way of life and of being church that may have been fitting in a previous era but no longer can draw resources from a radically changed ecology. Such congregations live off of themselves or, worse, cannibalize the resources left by a previous generation, such as an endowment. An *anxious reaction* would be to look to the church they once were or to a numerically flourishing congregation in their community. Realizing that they will never "be themselves" again, or envying the neighboring congregation, leaders in such congregations may engage in the renewal program *de jour*, trying first "natural church growth" (per Christian Schwartz) and then working for a month on becoming purpose-driven (like Rick Warren), without sustained attention or resources devoted to any direction and without ability to attend to their context in the present.[2] Such congregations look in the mirror and constantly see who they *are not*, which means they never deal with who they *are* and, consequently, have no clue what the mission is that God has called them to in *this* time and in *this* place.

Concern about size expresses people's obsession with the *past* (looking back at who they once were) and anxious concern for a congregation's *survival* (extrapolating from trends, as if the trend is destiny). But survival for the sake of survival is an unworthy mission for a Christian congregation. The issue to which congregations should attend is not size but *mission*, and mission is always particular to the congregation's context. *What has God called this people to in this time and in this place?* To whom and what, in this time and this place, should we offer our most precious gift—our full attention? Answering this question addresses issues of faithfulness and effectiveness. A congregation cannot answer this question if resources are dissipated by paying attention to size as a governing value.

Challenge: Preservation and Living Tradition

My wife and I have worked to preserve and to rehab the two homes we have owned. Both are 1920s bungalows, one California style and the other Chicago style. In preparation for our work, we consulted books on the bungalow, their history, heyday, and demise. We appreciated the Arts and Crafts movement's rejection of Victorian froufrou as we replaced lacy lights and pinks and baby blues with more period-appropriate earth tones. But still, we are a modern family inhabiting an old house. We had no desire to stay with the plumbing, electrical circuits, and other creature comforts that were common in the 1920s. So, while restoring some of the look and charm of a bygone era, we also updated and changed. Preservationists may desire to repristinate a lost form—if one is looking for a museum rather than a home. If a house is to be a home, it must be changed to accommodate the needs of contemporary families—and to enable that family to carry out its work in the home and in the larger world.

In the above section on size, I wrote about congregations that have, to put it most kindly, made it a part of their mission to preserve something of the past that they consider worthy. But preservation for the sake of preservation is not a gospel value. While we are thankful for the preservation efforts of ancient cathedrals and churches in Europe, as well as their younger American cousins, and while one can acknowledge that such places provide holy spaces that inspire the religious imagination, preservation is not an indigenous Christian value. Furthermore, not every church building is an architectural gem, or an example of how a church building should look, or a paradigm of careful craftsmanship.

Obviously, we also pay attention to preserving what we do inside our buildings. There are certainly timeless, or at least time-tested, elements of any tradition that are worth handing on from generation to generation. If this were not the case, then there would be no continuity between contemporary churches and biblical Christian communities. But I seriously question whether one generation in a congregation's life should try to bind subsequent generations to a particular kind of building, program, or worship style. Potluck dinners, late-nineteenth-century gospel hymns, church committees, receiving communion synchronically in the pews, four-part harmony, the eleven o'clock on Sunday morning worship hour—all of these are elements of tradition that do not *inherently* deserve our attention and resources. Sustaining them should be a choice.

Let's be frank: preservation in the church often means maintaining what *I* am comfortable with, with *my* history. Ecclesial preservationists cloak their desire in language of respect for the tradition. But in many of the Protestant churches I know, knowledge of "the tradition" does not mean the Christian tradition, the Wesleyan tradition, the Reformed tradition, or even the American subsets of any of these. To many preservationists, tradition means what I am comfortable with, what I grew up with, the architecture and hymn tunes and tempo and expectations of a disciple (or member) that make sense to me. Preservation means to build booths to house the relics of *my* Golden Age.

A long-serving and suffering pastor I know sent a letter to the congregation he serves (housed in one of the darkest buildings I have ever seen) that forcefully stated that either the congregation needed to make steps into the present day or the pastor would have to resign. The members responded with both outrage and support, although with much more of the latter. But the pastor's comment that invoked the most hurt feelings is when he, in a long list of comparisons between where they are now and where he thought they needed to move, stated that church potlucks should become more thoughtful feasts and that Jell-O salads should give way to more pleasing dishes. It was the Jell-O salad comment that almost turned the congregation against him. On the one hand, it seems like a petty issue that unintentionally distracted from the larger issues the pastor was trying to highlight, yet I can't help but wonder, how did Jell-O salad become an emotionally loaded icon in need of preservation?

While I have encountered some reflective traditionalists in the church, especially choir directors and musicians trained in the Western classical canon, most laity and clergy I've met who seek to preserve some tradition seem to protect the sacred object by denying its historical nature. The irony is frequently lost on us: we preserve tradition by ignoring history! For, whatever else history means, history means change. Change does not necessitate elimination of the old. But neither does respect for *my tradition* mean that it is not changeable.[3]

Preservation in the church is, I believe, an effort to fend off anxiety through sanctifying an obsession. The past as the past is not recoverable. There is no going back. One cannot fix what is wrong with the present by returning to the past. A desire to preserve artifacts of a "golden age" drains attention from the needs and opportunities of the present. Preserving a way of ecclesial life mottled with monuments to the past requires resources that could be otherwise engaged.

Anxiety fuels the desire to preserve. The future is feared. Life in the future will be worse than in the past, in the so-called golden age. The future represents a fall—falling away from original intent, falling away from flawless forms. If we use up our attention and attendant resources preserving the past, we think we can create a barrier to protect from the future and a discrete oasis in which we can live. In short, the desire to preserve, insufficiently connected to a reflective tradition, is killing many congregations established forty or more years ago.

What to do about aging buildings constructed in the twenty years after the close of World War II, as well as those that date from the earlier years of the twentieth century, demands significant attention today. This concern for dealing with deferred maintenance or modernization, and with the attendant concern of holding on to the ways of life that made sense when the buildings and congregations were built, consumes enormous amounts of congregational time, energy, and money. These concerns distract from fundamental questions about the *living tradition* received that congregations must pass on. Preservation should not be the issue. Handing on a living tradition—a growing and changing tradition—is.

Tradition, wrote Alasdair MacIntyre, is an ongoing conversation and argument about the good. It is a dynamic, living entity. A tradition changes according to the interests of the present inhabitants and conversation partners. Theologian David Tracy argued that traditions are ambiguous and plural, rather than always internally consistent and singular. This means that the Wesleyan tradition, the Reformed tradition, the Free Church tradition, the African American tradition, the Catholic tradition, and the Orthodox tradition are not truly *the* tradition. Each name represents a family of traditions, conversations, and sometimes-competing arguments about what is considered good, true, and beautiful.[4]

Rather than obsessing about preservation or anxiously preserving, congregations ought to focus their attention on receiving and passing on a living, spiritual tradition. I will say more about the content of that tradition in chapters 3 through 6. Here I want to emphasize that the process of receiving is an active reception, not passive. To receive and pass on a tradition does not mean preserving it without change. It does mean that we must learn the tradition well, make our theological judgments about its virtues and shortcomings, and change it as we embrace it in the only time we can find the Spirit's activity, in the only time we are given to live: in the present. After all, "The Sabbath was made for humankind" (Mark 2:27).[5]

Challenge: Technology and the Gospel Message

If ever the church faced a two-edged sword, with one edge cutting what and where you want and the other what and where you don't, it is technology. Technology is a marvelous connecting tool, a conduit for immensely helpful and inspirational information, that can and does enrich the ways we learn and find opportunities to connect. Technology also is demonic, flooding us with useless and harmful data, degrading us by tempting us to live at a faster pace than the replenishment needs of the human body require, and enabling us to shrivel our public spaces while we insulate our cocoons.

I am no Luddite, wishing to destroy the machines to which we have connected ourselves. Technology has been and will be an important tool in spreading the gospel. When I was a seminary dean, I encouraged faculty to learn to teach with newer technologies and to make decisions on using them based on educational goals. I reminded them that the book represents a form of distance learning: it allows a student to learn from a scholar's mind while residing halfway around the world from the teacher—or separated by centuries of time. The printing press represented a significant technology that was used to transform Christianity beginning in the fifteenth century. It is hard to imagine the Reformation without Bibles, books, and pamphlets. But technology per se is a *tool*. In an era such as ours in which the medium and the message are so closely tied, it is essential to pay attention to the ends and let those determine the means. *Technology cannot save.*

At the other pole from the preservationists are those who do believe that technology has salvific power. The thinking goes something like this:

> Look around this place. Grey heads everywhere you look. Our children grew up and either do not attend church or they attend one of those congregations that project all the readings and songs onto a screen. In those congregations, they use many more instruments in worship than we do. Rather than relying on a pipe organ and a classically trained choir (and our organist drags the hymns and the last person who could sing without warbling left us several years ago), those churches have a band, with an electronic keyboard and something like a karaoke machine to provide much richer support for congregational singing. When the pastor preaches, her words are synched with projected images, and sometimes movie clips, that illustrate what she is trying to communicate. I also know they have the latest duplicating equipment, software for their computers, smart classrooms, and a Web site where they make sermons available both as text and in streaming video. I know one place that even streams the service to the Web in real time. They talk about having a real congregation and developing a virtual one. How are we going to compete with them? If we want this congregation to survive longer than the next decade, we had better use some of those memorial funds to buy some equipment and learn to use it.

Now, a great deal of this statement *could* be commendable. Recognizing that different generations will receive the gospel differently, and that there are differences within as well as between generations, is important. But technique is no substitute for substance. And technology is a means rather than an end. I am concerned that technology is such a powerful force in our lives that we are distracted by its power and slip over into thinking that the technology will save rather than holding firm that we use technology to help communicate a saving message.

Technology represents both an obsession and an anxiety for the church. The former claim may seem counterintuitive. Doesn't technology keep our eyes forward-focused? If so, then anxiety might make sense, but not obsession, which fixates in the past. But I would argue that finding the right technological solution is an American obsession. To the extent that U.S. churchgoers participate in this wider cultural ethos, we participate in this obsession with technology. Believers in the modern myth of progress, the progressive betterment of human life through applied science, we look to technology to fix virtually everything, including the problems caused by our use of technology. As a people, we are much more adept at looking for the technological solution, which we trust will provide a relatively quick fix, than at formulating spiritual or moral solutions. The same congregation that can put together an IT plan may eschew doing the theological work that would provide the reasons and the message that the plan would help them to fulfill.

That technology represents anxiety seems obvious, especially for those who did not grow up with a mouse, joystick, or game controller in hand. In both church and seminary, I have seen very mature adults who regressed into "math is stupid"-type comments when challenged by computer-"assisted" teaching. But using communications technology also hooks the novelty-desire in our attention and routinizes our expectation that something new will be coming soon. Congregations that decide to move extensively into using computerized technology will have to fight the anxiety of being left behind by the latest advances.

The church does not need to be on the cutting edge of technology. The cutting edge is expensive and volatile. In the computer world, hardware and software quickly become commodities. Part of the cost of technology when it is first released is the "cool factor." Paying the cool factor premium is not good stewardship. Computers, peripherals, and software fall in price as they age, especially when the manufacturer releases a new version. Also, when first released, new versions of a product (especially in the PC world) are notoriously buggy. Let the commercial and military enterprises, which are the largest markets for many new technology products, test them. Again, it is good stewardship for the church to wait a bit before replacing "the old stuff."

If a congregation buys into the American value of owning cutting-edge technology, the investment is great, especially the long-term investment of keeping everything compatible and virus-free. Technology and its attendant costs can substitute for or distract a congregation from the more primary issue of promoting the gospel. If a congregation obsesses about its perceived past in a geographical community and is anxious about its relevance to younger generations, attending to technology may substitute for paying attention to a congregation's fundamental ability to communicate the gospel and to attend to any new thing that God may be doing. In chapters 4 and 5, on the practice of theology in a congregation and on other attention-strengthening congregational practices, I will offer means to grow in our ability to pay attention to just that.[6]

Challenge: Symptomatic Conflict and Suffering

A student was struggling to understand why the people in the congregation he serves can be so nasty to each other. His lack of understanding was not due to an inadequate definition of sin; as a recovering alcoholic, he knew well the depths of depravity to which a person can sink. But he had not previously encountered the daily, pedestrian nastiness, the backbiting and gossiping and generalized distrust. As we analyzed that congregation's culture in class, my teaching colleague asked, "Is there any history of boundary crossing, especially by the pastor, of acting out sexually with parishioners?" "I don't know," came the reply, " but there are a few people I can ask about this." He did. In the coming months, he dug his way back to an incident some twenty years earlier, of the pastor taking advantage of a teenaged girl. At the time, the pastor was moved to another congregation and the denominational official involved admonished all parties to bury the incident. They did just that, and that buried-alive incident added to and multiplied the toxins already in that congregation's culture. The congregation resided in an area where churches practiced shunning, and many of this congregation's families came into the church with the shame of being shunned. Shame added to shame and festered for decades. Leaders found their attention constantly distracted by symptoms of a deeper conflict and pain, yet they spent all their attention and energy on the symptoms.

Churches fight about issues such as carpet color and hymn selection for many reasons. Sometimes, one influential family wants to use the church as a personal chapel and insists that, since the sanctuary needs new carpet and they are willing to pay for it, they will choose the color to match their daughter's bridesmaids' dresses. But often there is a hidden issue, much more difficult to address. Sociologist Georg Simmel, one of the seminal writers on the subject of group conflict, argued that conflict is an essential aspect of group life. It can be used either to bind groups together, uniting against a common enemy, or to tear them apart. Give people something important to fight about, Simmel admonished, or they will pick something picayunish.[7]

It is also the case that groups attend to picayunish issues in order to keep the larger—more frightening—ones at bay. In church committee meetings, and maybe even in worship, have you ever thought, "Come on, you've got to be kidding. This is not worth our time. There are so many important issues. Why are we dealing with this trivia?" If you have, it is likely that the group was distracted by symptoms of something bigger. Unhealed wounds, unresolved abuse, and the fear of being exposed to massive amounts and depths of suffering keep smaller issues alive for unnaturally long times.

Why don't congregations focus more of their attention and resources on combating AIDS, hunger at home and abroad, domestic violence, all things that make for war, mediocre or failing public education, environmental degradation, the sexual exploitation of children and youth, and a culture that does not helpfully support singles or families? Why have the old mainline denominations decided (or fallen?) to deepen fault lines on the "issue" of homosexuality rather than on, for instance, how justice in the global market should influence the consumer practices of congregations and their members? Why don't we argue and debate and measure our success as congregations by focusing on our agency in transforming lives? Jeff Smith, the late "Frugal Gourmet" and a United Methodist pastor, used to quip about a "Methodist stove": it gets hot when it wants to rather than when it should. That is the case when we attend to symptoms rather than finding and attending to the systemic conflicts. We shovel away the droppings from the elephant in the room or spray air fresheners but either ignore the elephant or, if we are unaware of the elephant, hardly wonder why we spend so much time cleaning and freshening.

When we do not know or cannot acknowledge the elephant, it can engage our attention either as obsession or anxiety. Remember Shakespeare's Lady Macbeth obsessed with the "damned spot," which was not there but which represented the soul-stain from the murder? Unacknowledged or secret past brokenness has the power to affix a group in a past time. There are congregations that experience a traumatic event in their pastor's life—a divorce, the death of a child, a fatal heart attack, even a suicide. Such events, insufficiently attended to at the time, can hold a congregation in the past. When a pastor "leaves" a congregation traumatically and suddenly, the congregation may develop a coping strategy of "leaving" a new pastor as soon as the pastor is called, running through a succession of unhappy pastorates. In one case I know, the congregation's leaders swore that the pastors who followed a beloved pastor who had committed suicide all left on their own. That was, in a sense, true. But one could also argue that they fired each of their leaders from the outset in order to prevent feeling the trauma of being abandoned again.

Clearly, these kinds of traumas also have consequences for anxiety levels. A congregation might fear facing the future because it believes there are no more good leaders out there. But it does not take a pastor's suicide for a congregation to behave anxiously and to generate picayunish conflicts to stave off facing the elephant. How many congregations exist in ecologies where the toxins for their lives have increased markedly in the last few decades?[8] Congregations that hang on in high-crime areas, or in suburban neighborhoods too affluent and entitlement-oriented for their own good. Congregations that, based on their behavior (and despite their rhetoric and mission statements to the contrary), still hope that newcomers, resembling themselves, drawn to the same beat and tempo and presentation of the gospel that also attracted the current members, will stream through their door, wallets and hands at the ready. Congregations that function as if they still have the support of Christendom rather than acting within the reality that they are disestablished and live in a post-Christian ecology. Congregations that no longer know what to do, so they either do nothing or they try some of anything (natural church growth, radical orthodoxy, a seeker service, Taizé) for a brief time, without allowing sufficient time for anything to work.

Those congregations that try anything, and try it often, pressure their leaders to produce—NOW. Employed program staffpersons are particularly vulnerable as anxiety bearers and targets. Frequently, the pastor is scapegoated. Most of us would rather find someone to blame for our problems than to accept responsibility for them, akin to Adam in the garden blaming "the woman whom you gave me" when God asked him about eating the forbidden fruit. In scapegoating, the sins of the group—the disease—are attributed to one person. Youth don't attend? Rather than looking for reasons in a decades-long pattern, blame the pastor's age. Older members don't feel taken care of? Rather than looking seriously at the staff's recommendations regarding forming care teams, blame the pastor's time spent with the youth. Members don't feel motivated to go door to door in the neighborhood? Rather than addressing the issues of style or prejudice ("that's what Jehovah's Witnesses do") or theology ("my faith is a private thing, I don't want or know how to talk to others about it"), blame the pastor's sermons.

It is imperative for Christian congregations to engage real suffering with strength and hope. In order to do this, we need adequate energy and attention. When we fear that we do not have sufficient energy and attention, we tie up our limited resources with symptoms. In chapter 6, I suggest practices that leaders might consider that could make more energy and more attention available to deal with what really matters.

Worship Wars: An Example of All Four Challenges

The so-called worship wars controversy illustrates the distractions of size, preservation, technology, and symptomatic conflict. By worship wars, I mean that battle within congregations regarding, ostensibly, the forms of worship: music type (such as classical, gospel, or pop-influenced), beat, and volume; use of technology (do we stick with books or use projectors?); body postures (kneeling in prayer, arms lifted in praise); "reading" the Gospel (from the lectern, through dramatic presentation or dance); the sermon (delivered from the pulpit or from "down front," by one person or by a team). Occasionally in these controversies, combatants grapple with substantive issues. Often, however, I fear that fundamental questions such as "Why do we worship?" go unasked and, as is the case in so much of our entertainment-oriented lives, we debate on the basis of what pleases us rather than thinking hard about what is right.

Getting worship "right" should be a major focus of a congregation's attention. Worship is too important to the Christian faith for any community to be divided in worship and by worship. The center of the Christian community is named and sustained in worship. Old Testament scholar Paul Hanson's *The People Called* persuasively argues that, in the Bible, right worship is essential for right living. Hanson traces the concept of community throughout the biblical text. He finds a link between righteousness, compassion, and worship. Communities in the Bible, from early days, linked right worship to compassionate and righteous living. If a community abandoned the right worship of the God who led them from bondage in Egypt, then that community might also abandon its reason to be home for the "enslaved, the poor and the bereaved."[9]

The apostle Paul's imploring question to the Corinthian congregation should be understood as akin to the question of who and what is the center of worship: "Has Christ been divided? Was Paul crucified for you?

Or were you baptized in the name of Paul?" (1 Cor. 1:13). One could infer that Paul was horrified at the thought of being the center of worship. He knew that communities take the shape of the God we worship.

Worship is the central act of the Christian community. Theologian Lewis Mudge comes at the centrality of worship from a different angle.[10] According to Mudge, globalization of markets and communications has drawn together the earth's peoples. This drawing together more closely links our destinies with each other than has been possible in any other era. In the midst of these processes, God's spirit is remaking the people of God. God is calling the church, as part of that people, to discern and join the activity of God in the world; and the church cannot recognize the activity of God apart from engaging in right worship. Right worship educates our attention.[11]

And here, we know, is the rub. Here, at the point of discerning what constitutes "right worship," we become defensive and take offense. The issue of what constitutes right worship is as prominent today as perhaps any time since the sixteenth century. The issue of the character of the One we worship divides our communities. Conversing and arguing about the character of God and, consequently, about the people we are called to be, are worthy of our attention and energy. However, we often misdirect our attention to matters of size, preservation, technology, and other symptoms of dis-ease.

- *Size*: Worship is not *primarily* evangelism. It is not *primarily* a form of outreach. It is, *primarily*, worship of the Triune God. Because of the success, in particular contexts, of so-called seeker services, some congregations attempt to blend elements of seeker services into the community's Sunday morning service. Fine. But have we asked how either the present forms or the proposed changes enable congregants to worship God rightly and to be formed into the image of Christ? We could use the occasion of a congregation's numerical decline, and the absence of whole age cohorts, to learn not only about cultural differences between generations and between racial and ethnic groups. We could use these occasions to reflect upon what constitutes right worship.
- *Preservation*: Psychologist Robert Kegan and his colleague Lisa Lahey argue that, in and through organizations, people work not just to bring about the heaven they desire (the stuff that shows up in corporate mission statements). They also create walls and bulwarks to prevent hell from coming.[12] Congregations, located in an ecology that does not support that congregation's way of life,

can come to view the host culture as toxic. In order to keep the toxins out, a congregation tries to preserve its life by following a worship pattern that was fitting "in better days." To change and adapt to the culture would open the floodgates to the forces of hell.

Congregations arguing about music and worship could be cited as pure types of this insight. Currently, the preservationists' cause focuses on music. It is not fair to say that they appreciate the classical canon only. For the more educated preservationists, the issues are complexity and, occasionally, even theology. Good. But the issue should be the connections between a form of worship, our theology, and the potential of that form to shape us into God's people.

- *Technology*: Hymnals and Bibles represent technology. So does the sound system, including the wireless receivers for the hearing impaired. So do *any* musical instruments. The lighting and the window glass and other building materials—products of technology all! The issue regarding technology and worship is not whether we should use technology in worship—we already do. The issue is which technologies are appropriate, given the aims of worship. Which technologies help us worship the Triune God rightly? Which will help to form us into Christ's people? Theology, not anxious fascination with technology or attraction to novelty, needs to shape our conversation about which technologies are desirable.

- *Symptomatic Conflicts*: The worship wars bear symptoms of conflicts facing aging congregations. The key issues facing the church today are not about numerical size, or preserving a way of life developed in one context, or technologies used. Rather, the key issues are, first, regarding mission: what does God call us to be and do in this time and this place? Second, what is our living tradition? We should converse and argue about and celebrate and pass on a living tradition, which we have altered as we live in it and that will be altered by those who receive it from us. Third, what is the gospel and how do we teach it to ourselves, live in it, and proclaim it to those who do not know it? Fourth, it is time to identify the elephants in the room, both the one that is unique to our congregation (if there is one) and the ones that are there because of the society in which we live. To identify the elephants means to recognize, come face to face with, and give our attention to those who suffer. It also means to know the hope, the good news, that Christ has given the church to offer to the suffering. But we can neither attend to the suffering nor offer hope if our attention is distracted and filled with obsessions and anxieties.

The four distractions upon which I reflected in this chapter are expressions of what philosophers call technical rationality, meaning to try to solve a problem within the framework that generated the problem with the tools at hand. As you can tell by now, I do not think these technical solutions will work. We face what organizational development expert Ronald Heifitz calls *adaptive challenges*: we need to learn a different way of thinking and behaving.[13] In the next chapter, I begin to make the case for a different way of thinking, starting with attending to what attention is and the importance of the church paying attention to attention in order to strengthen our ability to see what God is doing—and to join in.

Conversation Starters

- What are the major obsessions (with the past) in the congregation's life? Where do you see them?
- What are the major anxieties (about the future) in the congregation's life? Where do you see evidence of them?
- Pay attention to one obsession or one anxiety in the congregation's life. What does the obsession or anxiety signify?
- Reflect on the following within your congregation:

  — Sense of mission
  — Your understanding of the tradition the congregation seeks to embody and pass on
  — Understanding of how to expre ss the gospel within your culture
  — Ability to be present with hope among those who suffer

Chapter 2

Attending to Attention

Being Present to God and Neighbor

When he was a child, my son Peter taught me something about paying attention. He might be chattering away, either to me or—seemingly—to whomever. Often, I could feign attention by saying "Ah huh, that's nice" while keeping my nose glued to the book in my hands. But sometimes Peter needed my best attention. He would bring himself in front of me, push down the book or the paper, then grab my chin. He would repeat, "Daddy, Daddy . . ." until my eyes met his and he knew he really had my attention. Sometimes parallel presence—two persons sharing the same space—is okay. But sometimes nothing other than real attention—eyes meeting eyes—satisfies the need.

What is attention? When it comes to offering a definition, naming what attention is is akin to what Augustine mused about time: we think we know what we mean until we attempt to define it.[1] In everyday usage, attention has several connotations. For instance, it is something we can "pay." The command to "Pay attention!" implies that we can direct our attention. Just as we value time and money (both of which we also claim to "spend" or "pay") highly in our society, we also value attention. By implication, we value that to which we give our attention. We also speak about "having" attention, as if it were some sort of commodity or thing. We also talk about "getting" someone's attention, meaning that we cause someone to notice what we want that person to notice.

We are aware that activities such as driving a car require a certain amount or quality of attention; using a cell phone, trying to still a screaming child, or attending too much to a billboard may distract one's attention sufficiently to lead to an accident. These examples of being partially distracted imply that attention can be given incompletely, can be divided, or can be of a greater or lesser quality. There is much concern these days about attention deficit *disorder* (or, more properly, attention deficit hyperactivity disorder, ADHD), which makes attention sound like something someone might not have enough of, or that there are healthy and unhealthy ways to allocate our attention.

This brief reflection on common usage raises the question, what is it that we are said not to have enough of? And how much is "enough" to do what? And why would someone not have "enough" attention? Common usage also assumes that we are capable of giving our attention to one thing rather than another, that we are capable of directing our attention, that we can choose to give our attention to—for example—writing a book rather than surfing the Internet, or listening to where your neighbor hurts rather than the evening's entertainment news. In order to address these questions about what attention is, let's look briefly at insights from philosophy, psychology, and brain research.

We Become What We Attend To

What is attention? Author and teacher Carol Zaleski writes that, in the ancient Western philosophical tradition, "attention was the capacity to be attracted . . ."[2] Within human beings there are reception areas, the desires. Desires attract us to certain objects. For the ancients, we become what we attend to; that is, we are formed by the things to which we are attracted. And, when we are not attentive to attention, we are de-formed by the objects of attraction. Plato worried about the educative and deforming power of music. Many ancient writers warned that we become what we look at. Numerous Hellenistic observers echoed Jesus' statement about the eye as the "lamp of the body."[3]

Early modern psychology shared ancient Western philosophy's conviction that we are shaped by what we attend to. William James, writing on the subject of attention at the beginning of the twentieth century, spoke of attention as an active mechanism, a sometimes involuntary and sometimes voluntary power of choice. According to James, attention is "the taking possession by the mind, in clear and vivid form, of one out of what seem several simultaneously possible objects or trains of thought. Focalization, concentration, of consciousness are of its essence. It implies withdrawal from some things in order to deal effectively with others, and is a condition which has a real opposite in the confused, scattered state . . ."[4] Attention is associated with selection and focus. Without attention, life is but a mess of stuff.

Modern experimental psychologists also investigate this necessary function of attention to *filter* and to *sort*. It is neither possible nor desirable to attend to everything, equally, all at once. In fact, if we did not filter and forget much more than we take into our minds, we would soon collapse under the "weight" of all that meaningless data. Argentinean writer Jorge Luis Borges, in a short story entitled "Funes, the Memorious," tells of Funes, who lived an unremarkable life until the day he was thrown from a "blue-tinged horse." When he regained consciousness, he found that he was crippled—and from that moment he remembered every detail of everything his senses took in. No differentiation of importance, nothing forgotten. Soon, he was drowning in detail. The author reflects: "Without effort, he had learned English, French, Portuguese, Latin. I suspect, nevertheless, that he was not very capable of thought. To think is to forget a difference, to generalize, to abstract. In the overly replete world of Funes there were nothing but details, almost contiguous details." In the end, Funes died of "pulmonary congestion," a symbol-laden death indeed![5]

Modern researchers debate how to define the phenomenon we popularly call attention. Some view attention primarily as a resource of either a fixed or an indeterminate amount; attention is something we can use. Others claim it is a capacity with limitations: We can attend only to a certain number of items before our attention is full.[6]

One of the interesting metaphors utilized by researchers is "bottleneck." We know that we exist in the midst of uncountable "data exchange opportunities" every waking moment of the day. As I write these words, a bird chirps outside my study window, prompting a mental image of the corn-on-a-stick my neighbor put up there for the squirrels to prevent their thieving from the bird feeder. I hear the buzz of my computer, note the brightness of the lamp, and enjoy the voices of the German Renaissance choir that arise from my CD player. The taste of coffee, the nutty smell of my oat bran muffin, the flitting thought of my doctor's appointment later this morning, the sight of the calculator that needs to move to the other desk, which reminds me I need to pay bills. All along I have been chewing my muffin and drinking coffee, swallowing, breathing, not noticing the warmth or chill of hardwood floor on my bare feet. Now, I could not attend to all of this at once. Nor could I attend to much of this at all and think about what I want to write. If I try to broaden the scope of my attention beyond a narrow range, I quickly overflow my capacity and produce a bottleneck: too many signals, not enough "bandwidth." I must filter out the vast majority of inputs in order to write.

The idea of a bottleneck and limited capacity to attend would seem to conflict with an often-used expression today: multitasking. That's a phrase we hear often, a claim that someone has this ability to do several tasks simultaneously, or a "competency" that an employer desires in an employee. How does an accomplished multitasker do it? Brain researcher John Ratey informs us that the human brain cannot multitask, if that means to perform more than one thoughtful operation at the same time. The human brain does not function like a computer, which can perform several or many tasks simultaneously (such as scan for viruses while I write). Some people (such as moms) are able to move quickly back and forth between tasks, not unlike the circus performer who spins plates on top of sticks: while getting a new plate up, the spinner notes that a plate on another stick is wobbling and will need to be coaxed back next. Ratey does allow that we have two kinds of attention, foreground and background. The former is our good stuff, that combination of attention and presence that approaches focus and that is essential for us to make decisions and to act with care. Background attention is something akin to peripheral vision—signals we know are there that may require foreground attention at some point (for instance, the reckless driver I note in my rearview mirror) or just remain an element of context (such as the buzz of fluorescent lights). But, in order to exercise foreground attention, we must focus.[7]

Focus, over time, shapes our brains. To a lay science buff like myself, one of the fascinating learnings from brain research is that the configuration of our brains is changeable. Scientists refer to this as *neuroplasticity*: the brain changes shape depending on our powerful experiences and on what we choose to learn. The connections between brain cells grow or diminish; paths are made and reused, depending on inputs and habits. When we learn to play a musical instrument, paths form. When we learn a new language, paths form. When we watch television day after day, our brains may be changing. What we see, what we hear, what we do, what we think about any of this—all these inputs are capable, over time, of changing the shape of our brains. The ancients were correct: we become what we attend to.

Our brains are prewired to dispose us more to some inputs than to others. Neuroscientists tell us that a developmentally "old" part of our brains, the hippocampus, disposes us to be attracted to novelty, to pleasure, and to avoid pain. Consider the vast majority of inputs from the screens to which we attend. How do advertisers get our attention? With what do they tempt? The new. The pleasurable. The pain avoidant or alleviating.

To summarize thus far: attention appears to be a capacity for attraction and for presence. We can be attracted to many different objects, depending on what we desire. And that to which we "give" our attention is that to which we are present. We cannot be present to everything or every-one all at once. Within our attention's capacity, as well as within its power (more on that below), we *select, receive,* and *construct.* Attention filters, either selecting or—in the case of being overpowered by a stimulus (for instance, an explosion, an exceptionally attractive person emanating just the right pheromones, an annoying spinning pop-up ad on your com-puter screen)—giving way to some inputs rather than others. Attention receives the inputs for processing. Through the selecting and receiving processes, attention constructs our past, present, and sense of the future. When we change our mind regarding an event, it is in large part because someone or something has convinced us to pay attention differently. For instance, in terms of national memory, for years a Euro-American per-spective informed public memory on the meaning of Columbus's coming to the Americas, but this has shifted as media and academic attention turned to the perspective of Native Americans or First Peoples. Or, as regards personal memory, consider the value many of us placed on paren-tal advice in our teen years as compared to the value we give to that advice when we have our own children!

Before broadening this discussion by turning to religion and spiritu-ality, I want to acknowledge that some scientists would be uncomfortable with how I have been describing attention, for I have been writing as if human beings have wills and consciousness that are more than simply the by-products of electric and chemical reactions in the brain. I have been assuming that we human beings can willfully focus our attention where we please, that we can train our attention, that we can even—to an ex-tent—change the shape of our brains through how we pay attention.[8]

The Ability to Attend

In addition to capacity and presence, attention also comprises a power, a faculty—specifically, the faculty of constructing one's past and present. In any given moment, a person—whether consciously or unconsciously—is selecting data from the brain, from storage (memory), and from current stimuli, in order to orient oneself to the world. This selecting is the basis for identity. Selection from memory also forms the framework for under-standing the present and anticipating the future. When someone compli-ments my appearance, if I pay attention to my childhood memories of being mocked for how I looked, I may be unable to receive that compli-ment; my attention is full with the memory of insults.

Such construction is mostly an unconscious activity. However, reli-gious traditions, both East and West, non-Christian and Christian, help us to see the power of attention and the value of working consciously to strengthen the ability to attend, which will enlarge our capacity to determine what we attend to. *If we attend differently, we will be changed.*

We often associate the desire and practice to strengthen our ability to attend with Eastern religions, especially Buddhism. Indeed, Buddhist meditative practices seek to focus our wandering attention and still the "screaming monkey" that our minds can be when we first attempt to be still. Meditators bring consciousness to attention. While matters of attention are often unconscious, through practice one can bring attention largely under conscious control. Eastern meditative exercises aim to develop our ability to see life as it is, to penetrate the world of appearances in order to see things, and ourselves, as they are, without the streams of thought and feeling through which we normally see and grab the world. The world, as it appears to the senses, is not the real world. Emotions—especially anxiety and fear—and various vices confuse our judgment and our perceptions. In order to attend clearly and rightly, one needs to see these emotions for what they are, to attend to them to penetrate their character, rather than to see the world *through* them and thus to see distortions.[9]

In the United States public mind, it is common to associate attentive practices with Buddhism and Hinduism to the exclusion of other faith groups. When Christians desire to learn meditation, they will often find themselves sitting in rooms sponsored by Buddhists, Hindus, or possibly by Eastward-looking Unitarian Universalists. One might find more secular "sits" at a YMCA. Even scholars tend to overlook faiths such as Christianity when studying practices of attention. The Dalai Lama and a group of Western scientists collaborated for over a decade to formulate a multidisciplinary approach to and program for understanding and managing destructive emotions. In *Destructive Emotions*, the text that reports these conversations, Christianity is completely absent.[10]

This absence of Christianity from conversations regarding practices of attention is regrettable. Christianity has a rich tradition of paying attention to attention as a primary spiritual discipline or practice. This tradition is not a museum piece or a dusty relic but is very much alive. For example, search through the Internet and you will find Christian congregations offering classes or groups in meditation, contemplative prayer, and *lectio divina* (a slow, thoughtful, and imagination-engaging method of reading scripture). I would like to see more of this tradition practiced within contemporary U.S. Protestant Christianity because it is a primary, historically-rooted practice of training and strengthening our ability to attend to the reign of God in the world.

Christianity and Attention

In the next chapter, I will deal with the subject of Jesus and attention. Here, I want to introduce a Christian theological understanding of attention. In making this introduction, I have a great deal of help from the tradition, which I sample selectively.

The *Philokalia* (meaning love of the beautiful or the excellent) is a collection of writings, spanning a millennium, that come from exemplary spiritual practitioners, especially from the Orthodox tradition, including some of the group known as the desert fathers and mothers.[11] The texts express profound insights into interpersonal and intrapersonal dynamics, based on a spiritual framework and what might be called a Christian spiritual psychology. Modern readers will feel both distance from some texts (for instance, how often the authors identify demons with virtually any ill) and immediate recognition in others, for the mothers and fathers are close observers of human behavior and of the inner life.

Common topics include attention, dissipation, attachment and detachment, and discrimination (between the good and the not-good). Three quotations give a flavor:

> Do everything possible to attain stillness and freedom from distraction. . . . If you cannot attain stillness where you now live, consider living in exile, and try and make up your mind to go. Be like an astute businessman: make stillness your criterion for testing the value of everything . . . (I, 33)

> Let us sit still and keep our attention fixed within ourselves, so that we advance in holiness and resist vice more strongly. Awakened in this way to spiritual knowledge, we shall acquire contemplative insight into many things; and ascending still higher, we shall receive a clearer vision of the light of our Saviour. (I, 47)

> If you seek prayer attentively, you will find it; for nothing is more essential to prayer than attentiveness. So do all you can to acquire it. (I, 71)

In these writings, attention is a power as well as a capacity. It is a power to ignore potential desires that keep us from attentive prayer, which is essential for paying attention to God. Akin to Augustine's statement that God has made us for God's self and that our hearts are restless until they rest in God, the monks understand God as the end toward which our lives should head. Whatever else Christian attentiveness is, it is our inborn capacity and our learned ability to pay attention to God, and, as Buddhist meditation exercises allow the practitioner to penetrate appearances, so Christian practices enable a person to attend truly and rightly.

Now, you may be saying, "Well, that sounds great but we have so many more attractive distractions today than in the fourth through the fifteenth centuries when all these pearls were written." Fair enough. We, in our consumer culture, are certainly assaulted by more external draws upon our attention than they were. We *may* have to work harder today to focus than a fourth-century monastic. But "may" is the operative word. Our allegedly external "demons" may be no more tempting than the internal ones with which the *Philokalia* authors contended. While attractive distractions exist outside the mind, the desire to receive the distractions comes from within, from dis-ordered desire and distorted thinking.

In the eighteenth century, Methodism's founder John Wesley published a sermon on dissipation, a word that he thought was interchangeable with distraction. Wesley's sermon exhibits close affinity with the *Philokalia* as he cites the connection between one's inner condition and exterior attractions:

> We are accustomed to speak of dissipation, as having respect chiefly, if not wholly, to the outward behaviour; to the manner of life. But it is within before it appears without: It is in the heart, before it is seen in the outward conversation. There must be a dissipated spirit, before there is a dissipated manner of life.

Also akin to the Orthodox ancients, Wesley believed that God is the proper center of a Christian's attention. Happiness is impossible for those whose attention rests elsewhere than in God.

> Our desires are dissipated, when they are unhinged from God, their proper centre, and scattered to and fro among the poor, perishing, unsatisfying things of the world.... We are encompassed on all sides with persons and things that tend to draw us from our centre. Indeed, every creature, if we are not continually on our guard, will draw us from our Creator. The whole visible world, all we see, hear, or touch, all the objects either of our senses or understanding, have a tendency to dissipate our thoughts from the invisible world; and to distract our minds from attending to Him who is both the Author and End of our being.

Wesley judges that there had never been such a distracting, disordered age as his own, in his own nation. Given the thoroughly dissipating culture in which we live today, his words may amuse—and they aptly fit our own moment:

> A dissipated age (such as is the present, perhaps beyond all that ever were, at least, that are recorded in history) is an age wherein God is generally forgotten. And a dissipated nation (such as England is at present in a superlative degree) is a nation, a vast majority of which have not God "in all their thoughts."[12]

Among more recent Christian authors reflecting attention, one of the most famous—and certainly most cited—is the French philosopher Simone Weil (1909–1943). Weil's discussion in *Waiting for God* begins with attention and detachment: "Attention consists of suspending our thought, leaving it detached, empty, and ready to be penetrated by the object."[13] Here, attention is an active power of the mind (voluntary) rather than the capacity for involuntary reception. In this, she is one with the spiritual traditions we have noted thus far. But Weil distinguishes her writing on attention when she connects attention with love and with suffering, with being lovingly attentive to those who suffer. "Not only does the love of God have attention for its substance; the love of our neighbor, which we know to be the same love, is made of this same substance."[14]

Attention is the substance of love. With this thought, Weil expresses the central premise of this book: attention is the most precious gift any of us has to offer anyone else (and, as I will write below, that any institution has to offer, too). To receive undivided, undistracted, compassionate, and truthful attention from another is a healing gift. It is also, clearly, a risk for the attentive one. Giving attention requires that "[t]he soul empties itself of all its own contents in order to receive into itself the being it is looking at, just as he is, in all his truth."[15]

> Those who are unhappy have no need for anything in this world but people capable of giving them their attention. The capacity to give one's attention to a sufferer is a very rare and difficult thing; it is almost a miracle; it is a miracle. Nearly all of those who think they have this capacity do not possess it. Warmth of heart, impulsiveness, pity are not enough. . . . The love of neighbor in all its fullness simply means being able to say to him: "What are you going through?"[16]

Based on Weil's work, I want to revisit the generic definition of attention I offered earlier. Attention is the capacity for attraction and presence. Spiritual traditions of both East and West also understand that attention is a power, an ability that we can harness and strengthen. From a Christian viewpoint, we can view attention as the ability to be lovingly present to that which is true—in the self, in one's relationships, in the world.

More precisely, as a Christian, I believe attention is the capacity and the ability to be lovingly and truly present to God and to neighbor. Attention is a *capacity*: it "holds" an object, it can be expanded or contracted, it can be empty or full. As a Christian, I believe humankind has a capacity to be attracted to and held by God. Christians believe humankind is created in the image of God and that we exist *by* the will of God and *for* the will of God. To play with Wesley's metaphor, we must be "hinged" to God. To paraphrase Augustine, we are restless wanderers until we abide in God. This God capacity is coupled with desire for God; through prayer and other practices, we cultivate our desire for God. But that desire can be distorted. We can and do desire that which is other than God to fill God's place. We might call this attraction to distortion a distraction. We could also call it idolatry.

Attention is an *ability*: it can be strong or weak, it can be strengthened or weakened, it can be focused or dissipated, it can be directed, it can penetrate. As creatures fashioned by a loving God and created for that God, our object in life is to love God and love our neighbors truly. We have that ability, at least in potential. But if we are to move toward our potential, we must pay attention analogously to the way God pays attention and to the things to which God attends. Attending akin to the way God attends is the essence of being an attentive Christian, or an attentive congregation.

Institutional Attention

Up until this point, I have been exploring attention in individuals. What does attention mean when applied to an organization such as a congregation? Surely, there are very significant differences. We may liken organizations to bodies and speak of "the mind of the group," but analogy is not identity. An organization with a billion-dollar budget, global presence, and thousands of locations has a much greater capacity to receive, sort, select, and use data than any individual. If attention is the capacity for presence, is organizational attention the sum total of what individuals in an organization are present to?

The clear answer is no. In order to understand what institutional attention is, we must pay attention to *organizational dynamics*, rather than to individuals alone, that are analogous to and different from the dynamics that affect individual attention. Systems theorists teach us that organizations, like organisms, are more than the sum of their parts. In describing a congregation's attention, we will have to examine dynamics, relationships, and processes.

Institutions Must Attract Attention

Institutions are in the attention business. Without attracting attention from customers or constituents, an institution, like virtually any other human-made object (except toxic waste and Twinkies), will die. If no one votes or runs for office, democracy dies. If taxpayers revolt and residents refuse to send their children to public schools, public schools die. If everyone has a freezer at home, no one requires ice delivery, and that business dies (or morphs into another business). If no one cares to raise children or form a multiperson economic unit, the institution of the family is in trouble. If no one is attracted to a congregation for a generation, that congregation will likely die. Institutions must attract and hold the attention of persons with resources that the institution needs. Institutions draw attention from people in order to attract the resources necessary for their lives. Unnoticed institutions die.

In order to stay alive and to attract attention to their products or services, commercial institutions spend a great deal of money. Advertising is the means by which commercial institutions attract our attention, hook into some desire (even if they must create the desire), and draw resources to itself. The Web site AdAge.com reports that, in 2003, the revenues of 457 U.S. advertising firms they surveyed totaled 10.66 billion dollars.[17] This figure probably does not account fully for the money institutions spend on consultants to learn whether or not their ads have the desired effect, whether the messages are reaching their target audiences, whether anybody is listening. Commercial enterprises invest heavily in being noticed and desired.

Organizational consultants Thomas Davenport and John Beck have written about institutional attention in their book *The Attention Economy*. They claim that attention has become the scarcest "commodity" in our society. There are so many ads, so many screens, so many images and sound bites, so much *data*. An institution's leaders must concern themselves with attention on two fronts: (1) capturing and holding the attention of customers and (2) managing attention within the organization. Here is how Davenport and Beck define attention:

> *Attention is focused mental engagement on a particular item of information. Items come into our awareness, we attend to a*

particular item, and then we decide whether to act or not. Attention occurs between a relatively unconscious *narrowing phase,*
in which we screen out most of the sensory inputs around us. . . ,
and a *decision phase,* in which we decide to act on the attention-
getting information. Without both phases, there is no attention.[18]

The new element in their definition is the *relationship* between attention
and decision: without deciding to act on the information, "there is no
attention." If we follow this definition, then, a congregation's attention is
a corporate act of selecting certain data, interpreting, deciding whether or
not to act, and—if the decision is to act—choosing a fitting action.

We have clues to what institutional attention is, then, by looking at
the actions an institution has taken. If we focus on an institution's actions, we see the processes involved in institutional attention. We can also
compare institutional and individual attention.

- Individual attention is largely serial; institutional attention is
  parallel. We learn from brain research that individuals can pay
  attention well to only one item at a time, especially if there is
  anything complex in the situation. Depending on their size, institutions can attend to many things simultaneously: different workers at different machines, different plants in different countries,
  different programs run by multiple persons in the same building,[19] different worship experiences yet the same congregation.
- Both individuals and institutions receive, filter, and sort data.
  Arguably, the filtering and sorting processes are more complex
  and difficult for institutions to accomplish well than for individuals because there are so many more data entry points in institutions: more people, more data-monitoring systems, more
  potential feedback loops. In recent decades, business and nonprofit writers have advocated for developing vision, mission, and
  values statements. Writers do not agree entirely regarding what
  falls under each of these headings. But there is broad agreement
  that institutions need to envision a desired future (attraction),
  gain clarity and keep focused on the institution's role in bringing
  about that future (strategic planning and action), and live true to
  a set of guiding values (daily filtering, sorting, focusing). Actually living from vision, mission, and values goes a long way toward functioning as an attentive institution, attending to the right
  data, with a right perspective, and leading to fitting action.
- In individual life, we focus attention through habit. Rather than
  having to think about and make choices every day when we rise,

a habit enables us to eliminate options we do not want to pursue. Because I want to control my cholesterol, I do not make a choice for breakfast each morning—I make oatmeal. Because I want the first new thought in my mind when I arise each day to be uplifting, I turn to scripture or to spiritual writings *before* I turn to the day's news. For the sake of my health and ability to do my work and enjoy life, I schedule exercise and rest breaks into my days as I would any other appointment (okay, now I am imaging my idealized world; except for my oatmeal, I am less than consistent in my other habits). In institutional life, habits take the form of programs. A corporate wellness program, a program for recruiting top-notch college graduates, a program for increasing customer satisfaction, a program for junior high youth—these are institutional habits which filter out other would-be options and focus attention and the use of other resources—namely time, energy, and money. Everything cannot be up for decision at the same time.

- One of the key indicators of where institutional attention is "spent" is money. How are the dollars attracted? What are the processes for deciding how money is spent? What is cut when income does not meet expectations? What names are given to expense categories? Where do the dollars actually go? To what extent are the budget and the expenditures attuned to the stated vision, mission, and values? If you want to know how an institution's attention is allocated, it is difficult to find a more revealing path than following the money.

- Above, I wrote about filtering. This action may be even more important for institutions than for individuals. It is certainly more complex because the amount of data and the number of streams of data can be legion. Virtually all corporations, both for-profit and nonprofit, keep data necessary to complete reports required by external agencies, such as the Internal Revenue Service, the Department of Education, or a peer accrediting association. These data may or may not be well-used by the institution but can consume a great deal of time and staff attention. What should leaders pay attention to daily, weekly, monthly, yearly? When I speak with laity regarding the ideas in this book, virtually every person tells a story about how difficult it is in their jobs to get to the work they should be doing and to focus once one gets there. The demands, and the data, overwhelm. Answering e-mail has become a major issue. Some companies make rules about e-mail usage not only to keep their employees working while at work but also to filter out distractions. Similarly, in "open door" companies, management may give permission for employees to close the door for at least an hour in order to strain out extraneous or less important data and to accomplish the task at hand.

In addition to the need for institutions to filter, some analysts look to institutions *as* filters. The late educator and media critic Neil Postman argued that institutions should help individuals determine what is important to attend to.[20] One could argue that news media have done this for decades. Granted. But the need for filtering grows, as witnessed by the growth of Internet portals and search engines and of accounting firms vouching for a Web site's information. In chapter 6, I will argue that the church should function intentionally as portal and filter for its members, as well as a major source of turning data into information—which happens when data is placed within an interpretive frame.

Institutional Attention Deficit Disorder?

Institutions seek to attract attention; they are in the attention business. They also face problems with the attention they have to give, for attention in institutions, as in persons, is limited. Intuitively, we know this is true. Whether we refer to the individual or to the collective, there are only twenty-four hours in a day, and thus limits to what an institution can reasonably expect from personnel (focus on that word *reasonably*) in terms of time and energy, since every day brings tremendous challenges in filtering out, sorting, and acting upon data. One of the reasons why many U.S. workers labor an incredible number of hours is because they cannot attend sufficiently to what needs attention within a more reasonable, and sustainable, number. Too much data to process, insufficient time spent evaluating and learning, more projects underway than can be completed well, fear of competition driving management to accept yet one more project, resources spread more thinly than success demands.

Scientists and mental-health practitioners debate the causes of attention deficit hyperactivity disorder in people. Many point to physiological factors while others attribute the disorder, at least in part, either to social conditioning or brain shaping resulting from a fast-changing, data-overloaded, screen-based, novelty-craving culture. Clearly, organizations do not have brains or minds, per se, in the same way that a person does. But few would deny that organizations have personalities! Institutions do not have brains per se, but they do have something akin to a *mind* expressed in its distinct culture.

In the previous chapter, I noted John Ratey's definition of ADHD. Among symptoms, he includes "addiction to the present," preference for immediate gratification, and inability to linger on a task long enough to evaluate and to learn from that task. Apply these symptoms to organizations. If a corporate mind or culture encourages short-term thinking, takes on more projects than the company can accomplish well, and declines to spend time evaluating and learning, then we could say that organization shows signs of institutional ADD.

What Is at Stake for the Church?

Ancients and moderns alike claim that what we attend to shapes us and profoundly influences, if not determines, how we interpret and give meaning to life's circumstances. For example, consider two people in the same congregation, a numerically large fellowship. One is a visitor from a large church who thinks the place feels cozy. The other is a member who has been concerned over the past year that the congregation is growing faster than her memory can keep up with, and is uneasy about growing too large. Two people, same place, attending to different objects, experiencing differently.

Another example: two people, both of whom have seen intense suffering in their lives. One has managed to use his suffering to deepen his compassion for others who suffer; he is a ready friend and counselor to many in the congregation who grieve. The other hurts, and in that hurt he is stuck. Others pity him but would never go to him and "burden" him with their troubles. Two people, similar life circumstances, attending differently, with different demeanors and effects on the people around them. Again: imagine two congregations whose buildings sit kitty-corner to each other at the same intersection. They share very similar economic and racial-ethnic profiles. Both face a changing neighborhood, with a steady stream of new residents who do not look like them. One congregation plans a welcome campaign, including developing new attractors for their neighbors and educating themselves in how to be welcoming. Members remember that their forebears came to the neighborhood from somewhere else and found a welcome; they have awakened to their responsibility to do likewise. The other congregation builds protection around their building and their hearts. Fear of the future is a theme that plays often when they gather. Two congregations starting with similar material resources but with very different frames of attention.

In each of these examples, how a person or a people attends may not be the only relevant factor in forming different perceptions. But who and what the church pays attention to have tremendous consequences for its life together and its mission in the world.

Who and what should the church attend to, knowing that what we attend to shapes us? The obvious answer for a Christian congregation is "God in Christ"—yet this may be less obvious, and more complex, than it first appears. In the next chapter, I will develop this "obvious" answer. In preparation for that development, please consider this question: *what is the nature of God's attention?* We have clues in many parts of scripture. Consider the story of Joseph's reunion in Egypt with his brothers who sold him into slavery: "Even though you intended to do harm to me, God intended it for good . . ." (Gen. 50:20). *God attends to accomplishing good in all circumstances.* In Exodus 2:23-25, after the Egyptians had enslaved their guests and the Israelites cried out to God, the text reports that God heard their groaning, remembered the covenant with their forebears, and "took notice of them." *God attends to those who suffer.* Jump centuries ahead; see Jesus writing his verdict in the dust regarding the woman caught in adultery (John 8:2-11). *Christ attends more to the sinner's need for release from sin than the crowd's need see the law punitively applied.* Finally, juxtapose several of the many scriptures that inform us how differently God "thinks": God laughs at the nations' plans for dominance (Ps. 2:4); God's thoughts are on a different plane (or in a different dimension) from our conventional ways of thinking (Isa. 55:8-9); or Paul's remarks that "Jews demand signs and Greeks desire wisdom, but we proclaim Christ crucified" (1 Cor. 1:22-23). *God attends in ways that subvert conventional, category-making human thought.*

Clearly, if the church attends to what "the world" attends, our attention will misshape us. Various theologians assert that the church should be a "contrast society," distinct from its host cultures. To an extent, I agree. Congregations should practice attending differently from our distracted and dissipated age. Christians can engage in focal practices (see chapters 5 and 6) that will help us be a contrast people. But what is the content of that different attention? In the next chapter, I will offer an interpretation of the subject of Jesus and his attention, exploring the relationship between his message to the church regarding the reign of God and his counsel to avoid attention's vampires: obsession and anxiety.

Conversation Starters

- Which are the primary issues, situations, and groups to which your congregation gives its attention?
- In your judgment, how adequate is the attention you currently give to each?

- If you could change something about the way your congregation allocates attention, what would you change?
- Discuss your congregation's "attention span."
- Discuss the assertion that Christian attention is the capacity and the ability to be lovingly and truly present to God and to neighbor.
- Discuss Simone Weil's idea that love is the substance of attention. If you were to use this idea to assess how your congregation attends, what would you conclude?
- Does your congregation engage in any attention-strengthening practices? If so, which? If not, which current practices might help the congregation strengthen its ability to attend?
- With your congregation and its leadership in mind, reflect on Beck and Davenport's claim that leaders must be able to manage their own attention and the attention of the organization served.

Chapter 3

Staying Present

A Meditation on Jesus and Attention

The Lord's Prayer, the Our Father, is offered up in hundreds of languages every Sunday by millions of Christians worldwide. Many of us memorized it in Sunday school or the like and utter or mutter it with little conscious thought. Some Christians think of it as the perfect prayer, asking God for neither more nor less than is necessary for daily life. Simone Weil practiced praying it with attention to every word until she found herself transformed by it. I have come to think of reciting it as my week's most subversive and radical act.

The prayer is subversive and radical because the foundational concept of the Lord's Prayer is God's kingdom, the reign of God, and it is Jesus' message about the kingdom of God that is the core of his teaching. In the miracles, in the healings, in all his teachings, in his action, and in his very presence, the kingdom of God has come near. The kingdom of God is the central focus of his attention. Joining the definition from the previous chapter of attending as Christians to the kingdom of God, I will now assert: *the church participates in the kingdom of God—which Jesus embodied and proclaimed—when we attend lovingly and truly to God and to neighbor.*

Again, if we the church take this prayer seriously, it focuses our attention as Jesus' attention was focused. This means that we proclaim our allegiance to the Lord, which surpasses our allegiance to any other ruler. The Lord's Prayer begins with confessing that God is the Father (*Abba*, a familiar form of address, as a child addresses her or his "dad") in heaven—the place of ultimate power and governance. This Father is holy, again distinguishing God from any earthly father. And then comes the first and governing petition in the prayer: "Your kingdom come, your will be done, on earth as it is in heaven." Reciting this prayer is the church's pledge of allegiance to the reign of God. Allegiance to every other power is secondary. In this kingdom, we have daily bread—the essentials for our existence. All debts, material and spiritual, are mutually forgiven. The evil one cannot distract us, because no power of any kind can compare with God's reign, God's power, and God's glory.

The church needs no "keys to the scriptures" other than this prayer. At the heart of Jesus' teaching, at the core of his mission, as the central object of his evangel, at the focus of his attention is the reign of God: what it is, where we should look for it, how we can access it, when it is, how should we act in response to it and as citizens of it.

In this chapter, using the Gospels, I hope to unpack and develop what it means that Jesus teaches us about the reign of God, about how to attend to God and to attend to neighbor, and that the church is called to attend likewise.

Paying Attention to Kingdom Rules

Jesus' teaching is based on kingdom rules rather than conventional wisdom. He often employs images and stories that have effects on us which range from giving pause to turning around our focus to converting us. Trusting in anyone other than God and God's kingdom produces disordered desire and anxiety, for only God is supremely worthy of our trust. Jesus' "politics," meaning his understanding of power and governance and rules, is based on the kingdom rules of compassion and justice, rather than on conventional wisdom or purity codes.

What is a purity code? Every society divides between clean and unclean, holy and profane, pure and soiled. We apply these rules to activities such as eating and sexual expression. There are animals or plants we will eat and others we will not. Not every ethnic or religious group has formal kosher laws, but we all discriminate when it comes to eating. Some sexual activities are considered good, within certain roles and rules; others are thought of as immoral or "dirty."

But we also apply our purity rules to people. Some people (or at least some roles people play) are considered "clean-cut" and respectable, "good people." We think of others as wrong, rotten ("he's a bad apple"), and—again—"dirty." Consider the comments made about immigrants or minorities where you live. In the Chicago area, where I live, groups in power have applied the word *dirty* to new immigrant or migrating groups for nearly two hundred years. When my grandparents immigrated to the Chicago area from southern Italy at the onset of the twentieth century, they were but two of countless Italians labeled as "dirty" when they moved into a decidedly non-Italian neighborhood.

Jesus' teachings, however, muddy such boundaries for the church. The effect of his teachings should cause the church to attend to how he sees the world rather than to be shaped by the prejudices of our day. For example, when questioned about clean hands or kosher foods, Jesus responded that it is not what goes into a person that defiles but that which comes from the heart and out the mouth (Matt. 15:17-20). In particular, Jesus resisted and rejected the labels that the self-appointed clean people and powerful people gave to their "inferiors." Women, children, yeast, mustard, Samaritans, tax collectors—all were considered unclean in some way by the good religious folk. But these are but a few of the things and categories of people that Jesus located on a different social "map" than did some of the religious leaders of his day. The kingdom of God, declared Jesus, is governed by a very different set of rules from the ones according to which we normally live. It is this alternative rule-set that makes Jesus' teachings so attractive and, simultaneously, so dangerous. The rules of the kingdom of God command the church's attention, just as they focused Jesus' ministry.

Kingdom Attention and Parables

In the Gospels, Jesus frequently redirects or converts his listeners' attention. The parables on Jesus' lips, and in the Gospel writers' hands, serve as powerful converting tools. Biblical scholar Bernard Brandon Scott, in his study *Hear Then the Parable*, defines parables as brief fictional narratives that refer to the kingdom of God.[1] Through the use of concrete images, Jesus teaches the church about the kingdom.[2] In fact, the kingdom is so decisive for understanding Jesus that Scott argues "the kingdom generates parable, which in turn generates Gospel." "In the Jesus tradition, parables are handles on the kingdom of God; they enfold and encompass the symbol. By means of the parable one penetrates to the mystery of the kingdom—but only in parable."[3] Parables are the primary form of kingdom-speech.

Without actually using the word *attention*, Scott describes how parables work to grab the congregation's attention[4] and direct attention differently from conventional ideas, frames, and word usage. The kingdom of God is an anti-kingdom, often invoking rules and images that overturn the way human kingdoms function. "To situate 'kingdom' in a discourse that begins with a woman taking leaven and hiding it violates the primary associations of male power and moral goodness, driving a hearer into symbolic disjunction."[5] In other words, Jesus' use of "God is like the woman who . . ." and comparing the kingdom to yeast, which causes organic things to rot, pull apart our normal mental constructions of what sounds right. In academia, we talk about teachers creating cognitive dissonance, ideas that clash with what we think is right, in order to provoke students to think. Jesus used cognitive dissonance extensively. To use a vernacular expression: through parables, Jesus messes with the church's mind.

The Kingdom of the Small and Unclean

When you think of "kingdom" or "empire," what images come to your mind? I think of symbols of power: great statues; a castle or stronghold; legions of soldiers prepared for battle to expand the empire or enforce the peace; both great works of art and great weapons, each designed to evoke awe in subject and conquered alike; laws and judges to decide what wrong-doing is and to punish it; wealth. I imagine lavish banquets for royalty and for visiting dignitaries. I picture a hierarchy of nobility over servants, with lots of the latter as compared with the former. I think of a center or capital, as well as distant outposts in conquered lands. I think of something past, or perhaps from today's Middle East, because "constitutional democracy" seems antithetical to "empire," which implies an emperor. And, with a few exceptions, I think of males holding more official power than women as leaders of government, commerce, the military, and religion.

Certainly, all of these images applied to the great empire of Jesus' day, Rome. For us Westerners, imperial Rome is the exemplar for what it means to be an empire. Its accomplishments were mighty and impressive. Its holdings were vast, enveloping the *oikoumene*, the whole inhabited earth (or so they claimed; this is the Greek word from which we derive the word *ecumenical*). The Roman empire built great cities, engineered bridges and aqueducts that are still used, and laid down or repaired miles of roadbed on three continents to move armies efficiently, which subsequently enabled wide-ranging commerce and—eventually—the spread of Christianity. Empire building is highly labor-intensive. A great deal of Rome's physical work of empire building was accomplished by tens of thousands of slaves who were captured in war and did everything from working the fields to building roads to educating the sons of wealthy men.

It is this entire world that Jesus, in his parables, subverts. Recall the prominent pictures Jesus creates regarding what the kingdom of God is like:[6]

- Matthew 22:1-14: A banquet to which none of the invited guests showed and which was then populated by the poor and the physically infirm (a reversal of the conventional "who's who" for parties).
- Luke 13:18-19: A mustard seed that grows into a shrub, rather than producing the great cedars of Lebanon, a symbol of "real" power. A shrub—think of it. God's kingdom is like the mustard shrub: very small beginnings, sometimes planted where conventional wisdom says it does not belong, violating our understood boundaries of what is dirty and what is clean (a reversal of the "shock and awe" tactics that empires use to create their own glory and to evoke fear in the conquered).
- Luke 15:8-10: A woman who searches for a lost coin. Comparing God to a woman's action was at least as scandalous in Jesus' day as it is in ours; the comparison subverts the depiction of God as male.
- Luke 13:20-21: A woman who hides yeast in a great mass of flour, leavening the whole lot. How often I have read this parable and yet, until now, did not stumble on the word *hides*. She acts clandestinely! And, since yeast promotes organic rot, in her day's mind-set, she has ruined the whole batch—a very large batch. Yet, the kingdom of God is somehow like this woman's secret action.
- Matthew 18:1-5; 19:13-15: Without becoming like a child, one cannot enter the kingdom. Who has less power than those peasant children who pressed around Jesus?

All of these word-pictures portray a kingdom very unlike Rome—or any other world power, for that matter. God's empire, God's kingdom, is, in worldly terms, an anti-kingdom. The way the world "does" kingdom is not God's way. In God's kingdom, the lowly are lifted up. In God's kingdom, the poor become wealthy. In God's kingdom, the unclean receive honor. In God's kingdom, the servants are the great ones. Is there any wonder why "the common people heard him gladly" or why this gospel was so appealing to Palestinian tenants oppressed by absentee landlords or by Roman slaves throughout the empire? Or why the philosopher Friedrich Nietzsche centuries later ridiculed Christianity as a religion for slaves?

The parables of the kingdom of God, and Jesus' parabolic actions that show us what "acting in a godly way" means in context, exist to convert the congregation's attention from worldly empire to God's empire. That is the way the parables functioned in the first congregations to receive the Gospels. The continuing conversion of the church to become the sign, instrument, and foretaste of God's kingdom remains the parables' primary function. Attending to the parables and Jesus' parabolic actions should cause us to revise our understandings of right and fitting action from our culture's ways to God's ways. In the following pages, I will explicate one parable and one parabolic action to illustrate what I mean.

Who Is My Neighbor, or Who Proved to Be Neighbor?

The parable of the Good Samaritan, as recounted to us by Luke (10:25-37), shifts our attention twice, once through cognitive dissonance and once by changing the question.

As I wrote above, cognitive dissonance is the experience of being presented with data that does not fit our mental categories: thinking the earth is flat and being presented with evidence that it is round; Albert Einstein, contemplating the evidence of how unpredictably matter works on the quantum level, objecting, "God does not play dice with the universe"; finding evidence of a spouse's affair when you believed this could never be possible; Moses encountering a bush that burns without being consumed; Paul and Barnabas in Acts (14:8-18) being seen as the gods Hermes and Zeus by the people of Lystra who did not have any other mental categories in which to understand the healing they witnessed.

When we encounter cognitive dissonance, several responses are possible. We can reject the new data as if it never happened. We might grow angry with the one who confronted us. We might "change our minds" (such an interesting phrase!—to change our minds means to change our mental models, to attend differently).

The *cognitive dissonance* in the parable of the Good Samaritan is evident in the pairing of the two words: "good" and "Samaritan." It is well known, and often preached in sermons on this parable, that Jews viewed Samaritans as anything but good. Half-breeds, yes. Apostate, yes. Traitors of God, yes. But good—no. First-century Samaritans were descended from Jewish-Babylonian families, "mixed" families that were a consequence of the exile in the sixth century B.C.E. Jews looked upon Samaritans as dirty, polluted, incapable of good. Rotten trees cannot bear good fruit. So, when Jesus tells a story of the mugging on the Jericho road with the hero being the Samaritan, he most likely evoked a goodly amount of cognitive dissonance within his hearers. How could the
_____ [fill in this blank with a category of people marginalized by

your community, someone you hate, a person you think is incapable of good] do good and be the ideal neighbor? Jesus reorients the congregation's attention from their conventional outcast category in which they placed Samaritans to the possibility that Samaritans deserve something better, a place in God's—and their—circle of care.

The converted question occurs in the story's frame in Luke, in its setting in the Gospel. The evangelist tells us that Jesus told this parable in response to a religious leader's questions. The lawyer (read "professor of theological ethics") asked Jesus which are the greatest commandments. Jesus kicked the question back to him. After the man responded that we should love God, and love our neighbor as our self, Jesus affirmed his answer. But then the lawyer, seeking to "justify himself," asked one question more, "And who is my neighbor?" In response, Jesus tells him the story and ends not with an answer but *with a different question.* Jesus does not answer the question regarding who is my neighbor. In conventional thinking, is not "neighbor" one who lives nearby, in my neighborhood? It is an attribute we give to another—"So and so is my neighbor." Why do we care about this ascription? If I ascribe you as my neighbor, then I scribe you within my circle of care. Deciding who is neighbor and who is not establishes boundaries of care: within this circle, I care. Outside of it, I don't care, or I care differently. Jesus gives no attention here to drawing circles or deciding who is in and who is out. Jesus' concluding question reorients the lawyer's attention from who is the neighbor to who in the story acted as neighbor. The concept of "boundaries of care" has vanished. Being neighbor is about how one acts—*being neighbor is how the church should act.* In conventional thinking, the neighbor is about social status or geographical location. In kingdom-of-God thinking, the congregation should attend to the stranger in a neighborly way. The shift in attention is from setting boundaries of care to acting with mercy when we encounter anyone in need. This is not the way nations attend and care. It is not the way *our* nation attends and cares. It is the way that Christ calls the church to attend and care.

Hospitality: Simon and the Woman of the Streets

The story of Jesus at table in Simon the Pharisee's house (Luke 7:36-50) is an example of Jesus' parable-like actions. By following how he attends to the woman, in stark contrast to how Simon attends both to the woman and to Jesus, we can learn much about kingdom attention.

Jesus reclines at the banquet table when a woman approaches. We are not told her name, only that she is a "woman of the city" and a "sinner."

(She is not Mary Magdalene, whom a sixth-century pope equated with the woman in Luke's story.) As she cries, wets Jesus' feet with her tears and wipes them with her hair, Simon—Jesus' host—is offended. He muses to himself that, if Jesus was "all that," he would know what kind of woman was touching him. Actually, the story amuses, for no upstanding woman would let down her hair in public before men and do what this woman did. Every man at the table knew that the woman was "a sinner"; divine intuition was superfluous and overkill! However, Jesus did turn his divine intuition in Simon's direction. In doing so, Jesus directs the church's attention, along with Simon's, to a very different way of viewing the woman's action and his host's unfitting response to her as well as Simon's marginal treatment of Jesus.

Simon, acting in the stead of many of us good religious sorts—the folks who often make up a congregation—looked at the woman and saw only the offense against good morals and good judgment. Jesus saw a woman exercising costly hospitality. The late theologian Henri Nouwen, in his excellent book *Reaching Out*, wrote that hospitality is making room in your life for that which is not you without requiring that it become like you.[7] In order to be hospitable, we need to make room in our attention for the other, to become available to the other. The woman made herself as available to Jesus as she could. She was completely attentive to him. She attends to Jesus as the church ought to attend.

Jesus turns to look at the woman and addresses Simon (the congregation)—surely a sign of deep respect for the woman and a criticism of Simon. As he gazes into the woman's face, Jesus contrasts Simon's neglect of offering water to wash upon entering his home with this woman's act of cleansing his feet with her tears, Simon's lack of a greeting kiss with her continual kissing of his feet. In the parable of the two debtors told within this story, Jesus flips Simon's unspoken criticism of the woman back onto him. Simon, and not the woman, has acted offensively. The woman, not Simon, has been lovingly present, has acted as host and neighbor. This nameless woman attended well. Simon did not.

Jesus turned his face from Simon to the woman. Symbolically, he also turns the congregation's face to attend to outcasts as he attends to outcasts. Neither Simon's standing nor the woman's lack thereof is the correct object of the congregation's attention. Her hospitality to Jesus, Jesus' hospitality to her, and Simon's lack of hospitality is the object. The church ought to attend to Jesus with the courage and hospitality that the woman extended to him, and the church ought to attend with courage and hospitality to outcasts like this woman.

The Sermon on the Mount

Parables are Jesus' primary form of teaching about the kingdom of God. One of the other places where the kingdom is cogently presented is in what some commentators have termed the Christian "constitution": the Sermon on the Mount (Matthew 5–7). The Sermon on the Mount is one of the most recognized section titles in the Bible, but not as many people are able to identify it as the place to find the Beatitudes, the Lord's Prayer, teachings on divorce or false prophets, Jesus referring to his hearers as "you who are evil" (in contrast to God's goodness, 7:11), or the teachings on anxiety and attending to the reign of God. Before I turn my attention to a portion of the Sermon, I will set up the discussion by commenting generally on the Sermon and attention.

Chapters 5–7 of Matthew, which comprise the Sermon, consistently require the listening congregation to refocus attention from human ways to God's ways. Consider the following examples:

- Most of the "Blessed are"s in the Beatitudes defy conventional wisdom: the meek will inherit the earth; the kingdom belongs to the poor in spirit; mourners are blessed; the kingdom belongs to the persecuted.
- In the second half of chapter 5, the sequence of "You have heard it said" (meaning it is written in the Torah, the books of Moses) . . . "but I say," includes teachings on murder and anger, adultery and looking lustfully, divorce, swearing oaths, responding to evil with good, and loving your enemies. In each case, Jesus rechannels the congregation's attention from outward and conventional observance of Torah to a deeper principle that, at times, overturns conventional interpretation and practice.
- In chapter 6, in contrast to the way the good religious folk practiced their piety—outwardly, in order to receive human praise—we are told to practice alms giving, prayer, and fasting, but the congregation should shift attention from seeking human praise to seeking God's reward of favor.
- In chapter 7, Jesus catches the congregation's attention with a series of vivid pictures, even hyperbole: a person walking about with a great log protruding from her eye, yet attempting to point out the speck of dust on someone else's character; "evil" parents who yet know better than offering their children stones or serpents rather than food; narrow and wide gates; religious folks draped with a sheep's fleece but baring wolf-like

teeth; grape clusters on thorn bushes; a McMansion builder watching his sand-anchored home crumbling in a storm.

Anxiety and Kingdom Attention

In the first chapter, I wrote about anxiety as one of the two vampires of attention. Anxiety is born from a sense of threat, especially a threat to one's existence. I also wrote there about four anxiety-producing circumstances in the church's life today: (1) congregational size and getting handles on mission; (2) anxiety about learning to present the gospel through technology and seeking clarity regarding the content of the gospel; (3) making decisions about the heritage the church needs to pass on without getting mired in traditionalism; (4) dealing with massive local and global suffering with a word of hope, rather than spending out the church's attention and energy on distracting conflicts. In each of these circumstances, there are clear threats to many congregations' existences. Obviously, we can add other threats! Clergy scandals, the cost of health insurance and pension benefits for employed leaders, the inability of many mainline congregations to reach out to newer immigrant groups, talk of denominational splits, how to pay for clergy education (as well as what kind of education is fitting for today's and tomorrow's leaders), millions of dollars of deferred building maintenance. Any and all of these circumstances evoke anxiety in the church. Matthew's context for 6:25-34 creates a fitting prologue to understand how to dissipate anxiety and focus attention: be mindful of what you attend to, of who you are devoted to.

Matthew 6:19-34 was written for congregations in such a time as this (plus many more, in other contexts and cultures). These verses are the Bible's longest, most sustained discussion of anxiety and its antidote: trust grounded in right attention.[8]

What is treasure to you, church, and where are you storing it? What in your world does your eye, your lamp, cast light upon? Every church serves someone or something. Whom do you serve? Matthew 6:19-24 puts these questions to us. Let's briefly unpack these verses.

Where your treasure is . . .

Those of us who have possessions find it very hard not to be possessed by them, as if they are extensions of ourselves. In a sense, they are. If we purchase something, we use money. Money represents that for which we have exchanged our life energy: we "spend" our time and energy and are given money in return.[9] We turn around and use that expression of our life energy to buy something; that something now represents part of our life.

Through our energy, we acquire; the possession therefore represents spent life energy. Or, if someone gives us a gift, that gift represents the giver and their relationship to us. We are constituted, largely, by our relationships. Therefore, possessions we obtain as gifts also represent extensions of ourselves.

The problem with possessions is not having them but being attached to them. Possessions are a problem when they possess us. When we are attached to our possessions, which are vulnerable to "thief and moth," we may become devoted to them—not only the ones we have but also our power to obtain more—and thus expose our souls to theft and parasites. One of the misfortunes in my older son's life occurred when someone broke into his rented house and stole a football thrown to him by the late, great Chicago Bears running back Walter Payton. That football held a great deal of meaning for him. Losing it hurt him deeply. Vicariously, it hurt his family. If I owned that football and someone pilfered it from me, I would have felt much the same as my son did, and still does. It is difficult to own and value something and remain "detached."

Where your treasure is, there is your heart. Jesus both informs us of the relationship between treasure and heart and teaches us about true attachment. Seek treasure in heaven. This command is a variation of "seek first the kingdom of God" (v. 33). Appropriate attachment is to that which cannot be taken away and to that which can dissipate our anxiety because it is the only house not built on sand. What difference would it make for our congregational conversations about tradition and heritage and the gospel that we ought to pass on if we paid attention to where our heart is—and made certain it is attached to that which moth and rust cannot corrupt?

The eye is the lamp of the body . . .

For almost the last ten years, I have noticed how important the quality of light is to my ability to see. My ability to see at night and in low light has declined significantly. I prefer not to drive on ill-lit roads after nightfall. I can become highly frustrated when I endeavor to plug the cables and wires into our TV or music system, since manufacturers design their labeling for young persons with very good eyesight! The lettering is too small and, without a flashlight, I simply cannot see what I am doing.

At about the same time as I noticed this decline in my ability to see in low light, I also made my first visit to Santa Fe, New Mexico. I immediately discovered and understood what so many artists speak of: the quality of the light there. The sun in the high desert illumines the colors of the soil, the sky, and the mountains (both the day color and the sunset color, which earned one range the name *Sangre de Cristo*—the blood of Christ). The light is crisp and clean. We would not see those colors without that high-quality light. Seeing well, seeing truly, requires good light.

Jesus' words about the eye as lamp may reflect both first-century biology (how the eye functions in the body) and philosophy (the analogical meaning that we can draw from biology to how to live life well). Here, I am concerned about the latter. If the eye is the body's lamp, then the eye is a key to how we attend. How good is the light that our lamp emits? How well does it illumine our paths? Where do we turn it? Earlier in the Sermon (Matt. 5:29), using the metaphor of eye somewhat differently from our text here, Jesus warns us that it is better to tear out one's eye than to take in evil thoughts through it. But, whether the eye is receptor or cause of evil thoughts ("If your right eye causes you to sin . . ."), or is the lamp for our paths, the eye is a primary means of attending. What do you see? How sound is your sight? Do we cast light on our troubles, on tomorrow's cares, on what is missing? Or do we, the church, seek signs of the kingdom like the woman searching for the lost coin, bringing the lamp into dark and neglected corners in service of finding the treasure that may await us there? When we engage in conversation about our mission as a congregation in this place, what if we searched for God's reign in our communities like the woman searching for that coin?[10]

Whom do you serve?

As freedom-loving Americans, especially given our own history of slavery and indentured servitude, and despite attempts publicly to redeem the word *servant* in recent years (for instance, Robert Greenleaf's *Servant Leadership*[11]), the concept underlying "No one can serve two masters" is off-putting. If I understand what the words imply, then one meaning is that *everyone serves* something or someone. To use the late theologian Paul Tillich's language, we all have ultimate concerns—a concern higher than any other—and that ultimate concern, functionally, is god for us. That god could be a woman or a man, a role, a bottle, a particular possession, the pursuit of power or wealth, and a numberless variety of other deities. Each of us devotes our lives to serving some end. Everyone serves.

John Wesley compared and contrasted what it means to serve God or mammon. Serving either involves *trusting, loving, resembling,* or *obeying.* Serving forms us. Read what Wesley writes about "resembling":

> Now God is love: Therefore, they who resemble him in the spirit of their minds are transformed into the same image. They are

merciful even as he is merciful. Their soul is all love. . . . Yea, they are, like Him, loving unto every man, and their mercy extends to all his works.

To resemble, to be conformed to . . . mammon; to have not only designs, but desires, tempers, affections, suitable to those of the world; to be of an earthly, sensual mind, chained down to the things of earth; to be self-willed, inordinate lovers of ourselves; to think highly of our own attainments; to desire and delight in the praise of men; to fear, shun, and abhor reproach; to be impatient of reproof, easy to be provoked, and swift to return evil for evil.[12]

If we come to resemble whichever god we serve, is there then a relationship between serving and attention? Clearly, we attend to where we "devote" time, energy, and money. A congregation's ultimate concern certainly orients and organizes attention. In a sense, all gods are jealous; devotion to each involves specific rules, roles, and practices. The servant who tries to serve multiple "ultimates" at some point will incur the "wrath" of one god or the other. If staving off the past is a primary value that a congregation tries to serve, or if it serves guilt in hopes of producing better stewardship, or serves the value of being nice rather than of being kind or just in order to avoid real conflict, will not such congregations be misshaped through their service?

Do Not Be Anxious

Jesus' teaching on anxiety and its antidote, trust in the reign of God, came in anxious times. Scholars term the late Roman empire the "age of anxiety." Anxiety was a prominent topic in their written record. The authors of these writings united in believing that one could not be anxious and happy at the same time. In this literature, New Testament scholar Hans Dieter Betz[13] identifies three subthemes, each of which is reflected in Matthew's text:

- People feel anxious in response to many circumstances, some of which seem reasonable and others that do not.
- The human condition *is* fragile; anxiety will plague us all our days.[14]
- God is fundamentally good and provides good within creation. Even though sin sullies the world, God has not abandoned it or us. While this theological concept (providence) is not explicit in our passage, it undergirds the whole.

When scholars find parallels between the Bible and other literature in the ancient world, as we find regarding this text, they ask what, if anything, sets the biblical text apart. In this case, the distinction is clear, with 6:33 providing the key: "Strive first for the kingdom of God and his righteousness, and all these things will be given to you as well" (NRSV). Attention filled with the kingdom of God will exclude life's everyday anxieties.

Okay. That *sounds* wonderful. But is it true? Can we really live without anxiety? Can we really live without concern for food, clothing, shelter—the very necessities of life that are included in the Lord's Prayer's petition to "give us this day our daily bread"? Is not this vision of the world romantic at best, or even deluded?

This is a serious question that reflective people of every age must consider. To be honest and blunt, I decided to attend to this text for this book because I need to learn from it. This has always been a hard passage for me. In my own life, my "default" way of attending often is to hold up an ideal template of "the way life ought to be" as I scan or examine any situation. By employing this ideal template, I tend to notice first what is missing and how the present falls short of my ideal. I make dinner. The appetizer is fine, the salad is very good, the main course is outstanding—but the dessert did not turn out properly. While my guests thoroughly enjoyed themselves, I finish the evening smarting a bit because the partially "failed" dessert grabs much of my attention. I teach a course and receive my student evaluations. All but one evidences great appreciation for the course. Which one do you think expands to fill my attention? With the ideal template as my meaning frame, I notice discrepancies between ideal and real, rather than appreciation for everything that was and is good. Certainly, if one looks for departures from the ideal world, one need not look far! War, poverty, hatred, hunger, stupidity and ignorance, ugliness, natural disaster, disease, and everyday irritated meanness—just for starters. If you look for what is lacking or missing in this world, in your congregation, in your family, with your spouse, in your soul, you will undoubtedly find it.

From conversations with friends, congregants, and students, I know I am not alone in my default response. Many others are burdened with this *anxiety sickness*. Yes, I think an attitude such as the one I am trying to diminish in my own life is an anxiety sickness. In chapter 2, you may recall that I wrote about the dynamics of attention, attraction, and desire. In the ancient Greek and Roman world, attention was understood as the capacity to be attracted. Attention is ordered by our desires. Well-ordered desire leads to attending well, to fulfillment or happiness, to a tranquil mind free from distraction and anxiety. Disordered desire warps our attention and causes us to grasp for our security in objects that cannot give us the security we seek. The perfect congregation, the perfect pastor, the perfect parishioner, the perfect youth ministry program, the perfect Christmas pageant: an attempt to derive meaning from any of these will disorder our lives, for *we were not made by and for any of these.* Nevertheless, how much of the world we see around us is built upon disordered (sick) desire and attention? The first audience for the words, "Do not be anxious about what you will wear," may have owned nothing beyond what they wore daily. But we stand in front of closets packed with clothes, drawers overflowing, with boxes and bags in storage, and declare, "I have nothing to wear." We might open a stocked refrigerator or pantry, after having eaten an hour before, and complain, "There is nothing to eat in this house." How different from the first audience, which may have been endemically hungry and for whom food was only intermittently available!

Well, to quote a TV psychologist personality, one might ask, "So, how's that working for ya?" How is life working for those of us who order our lives according to our culture-shaped desires, attracted like moths to the flame?

We Are Not Alone

We should take heart, or at least find a community of fellow sickies, as we consider portions of sermons preached in other times and days regarding "be not anxious."

John Chrysostom (4th century):

Nothing brings so much pain to the spirit as anxiety and cark [care or burden]. . . . Has not every day a burden enough of its own, in its own cares? why then do you add to them by laying on those that belong to another day?[15]

Martin Luther (16th century):

Is it not a great shame that the Lord makes and presents to us the birds as our teachers, that we should first learn from them? Shame on thee, thou loathsome, infamous unbelief! The birds do what they are required to do; but we not. In Genesis 1, 28 we have a command that we are to be lords over all God's creatures; and the birds are here our lords in teaching us wisdom. Away with godless unbelief! God makes us to be fools and places the birds before us, to be our teachers and rule us, in that they only point out how we

serve mammon and forsake the true and faithful God....It seems to
me, this is disdain that is commanded, that the flowers stand
there and make us blush and become our teachers. Thank you,
flowers, you, who are to be devoured by the cows! God has exalted
you very highly, that you become our masters and teachers.[16]

John Wesley (18th century) also either knew anxiety well firsthand or was
a keen observer of how it works on others (from my reading of Wesley, I
would surmise he was both, at least in particular seasons of his life). I
quote at length because his words sound so contemporary:

> What [Christ] here condemns is, the care of the heart; the anxious,
> uneasy care; the care that hath torment; all such care as does hurt,
> either to the soul or body. What he forbids is, that care which, sad
> experience shows, wastes the blood and drinks up the spirits;
> which anticipates all the misery it fears, and comes to torment us
> before the time. He forbids only that care which poisons the bless-
> ings of to-day, by fear of what may be to-morrow; which cannot
> enjoy the present plenty, through apprehensions of future want.
> This care is not only a sore disease, a grievous sickness of soul,
> but also a heinous offence against God, a sin of the deepest dye. It
> is a high affront to the gracious Governor and wise Disposer of
> all things; necessarily implying, that the great Judge does not do
> right; that he does not order all things well. It plainly implies, that
> he is wanting, either in wisdom, if he does not know what things
> we stand in need of; or in goodness, if he does not provide those
> things for all who put their trust in him.[17]

Much closer to our own day, Dietrich Bonhoeffer wrote *The Cost of Discipleship*, a modern classic in theology, ethics, and spirituality.
Bonhoeffer structures the book as an extended teaching meditation on
the Sermon on the Mount. For him, the command to "be not anxious"
reflects the heart of the gospel: trust in God as God is known through
Jesus Christ. Those who trust have no need for anxiety. Those who do not
trust will always be anxious. Bonhoeffer connects the daily-ness of the
Lord's Prayer with this passage: trust that our petition for our daily bread
will be fulfilled. Furthermore, as Israel in the wilderness could gather
manna only on a daily basis, in a like manner we must learn to trust
God's provision in this day. The kingdom of God is always near—in the
present. Bonhoeffer encourages us not to assume God's burden of providing. Life is a gift; trying to turn that gift into fruits of our own labor assumes God's burden.

> We have here either a crushing burden, which holds out no hope for the poor and wretched, or else it is the quintessence of the gospel, which brings the promise of freedom and perfect joy. Jesus does not tell us what we ought to do but cannot; he tells us what God has given us and promises still to give.[18]

Is God trustworthy? That is one way of asking the question: is trustworthiness an attribute of God? The other way of asking the question is this: do you, as a congregation, trust that God is trustworthy? Anxiety in people can be rooted in more than one cause, including biochemical. In no way am I suggesting here that one needs only to decide to trust God and all anxiety would disappear like fog banished by the sun. But, regardless of the sources or causes of anxiety, one part of a better way to live is spiritual and theological. To paraphrase Bonhoeffer, anxiety is an expression of practical atheism. If we seek to live as disciples, seeking first the kingdom of God is the only way to live. Otherwise, we do not have sufficient attention or energy to live into our calling.

Conclusions: Strive First for the Reign of God

Jesus of Nazareth's core message was, "Repent, the kingdom of God is at hand." His teaching, healings and miracles, calling out and equipping disciples, preaching, acts of boundary-breaking hospitality and righteous indignation—all these should be interpreted as expressions of the kingdom. He prayed for the kingdom, proclaimed the kingdom, taught how the kingdom differed from the empires his people knew all too well, recruited for the kingdom, vividly imaged the kingdom, and died for the kingdom. Today, popular authors admonish us to keep "first things first" and establish "the main thing [as] the main thing." For Jesus of Nazareth, the kingdom of God is the first thing, the main thing. "Strive first for the kingdom of God . . ."

What does this mean, to seek first the kingdom? To paraphrase a contemporary expression, this question is akin to asking, "What *did* Jesus do?" (WDJD, rather than "What *would* Jesus do?") As it was with Jesus, so with us: the kingdom should be the primary object of the church's best attention. Where is God at work in our world? After praying the Lord's Prayer, imploring God for the kingdom to come "on earth as it is in heaven," we should scour the papers and our daily pathways for signs of God's activity, to which Jesus gave us many clues: look for mustard seeds (small things), women hiding yeast (in unlikely places), and outcasts proving to be neighbor (extraordinary yet everyday actions of hospitality and compassion). We should look for where signs of hope, however small, are offered to those who suffer: good news for the poor, release for the captive, healing for all manner of disease, liberation for the oppressed (Luke 4:16-21). We should look—and join! We should look for God's Swiss-cheesing work on our social boundaries with which we separate and protect ourselves from people we do not know or do not like. All this is what Jesus looked for, pointed to, proclaimed, and gave his life to. If this is what Jesus did do, then we have at least some compass directions for what Jesus would do.

A note of confession and a limitation: this interpretation of who Jesus is and what his ministry means for the contemporary church in North America is just that, an interpretation. If I had developed this chapter attending primarily to how Jesus is presented in John's Gospel, or from the perspective of the church in India, or through the frame of the ecumenical creeds of the church, or from the perspective of one who believes politics and religion should be as separate as church and state, Jesus and the reign of God would have looked different from the portrait I have painted here. Not completely different, but different nonetheless.

The great humanitarian and missionary Albert Schweitzer was also a biblical scholar. At the turn of the nineteenth into the twentieth century, he wrote *The Quest for the Historical Jesus*.[19] In this work, he surveyed the nineteenth-century biblical scholars' and historians' interpretations of Jesus as they worked with the latest tools of so-called "higher criticism" to uncover who Jesus *really* was and what he might have *really* said. Schweitzer's conclusion was that, in each case, the scholars' conclusions about the historical Jesus were none other than the *historian's* Jesus. Each scholar, attending to the data with their own framework and values, created as much—or more—a portrait of themselves as they did Jesus of Nazareth.

It would be wrong to conclude that we should ignore the scholars—just give me "the Bible and my Jesus." This statement is false, unless one acknowledges that "my" Jesus is an *interpretation*. We, the church, will *always* bring a framework to reading the text that will affect what, and who, we find there. We will always bring, implicitly or explicitly, interpretation. We will always bring, implicitly or explicitly, theology.

Theology matters. It is an essential discipline for the church. As it is said that war is too important to be left to the generals, so it is that theology is too important to be left to professional theologians in seminaries, in colleges and university religion departments, or even to the clergy. Theology needs to be a congregational discipline and practice. After the practices of worship and prayer (see chapter 5), theological reflection is the most essential practice to enable Christian communities to attend well. Theological reflection brings Jesus' teachings and actions regarding the kingdom of God and helps the church to attend lovingly to God and to neighbor today. In the next chapter, I hope to illustrate what difference attending to theology and attending through a theological perspective can make in a congregation's life.

Conversation Starters

- Talk to one another about your experience with the Lord's Prayer. When did you learn it? Who taught it to you? What meaning does it have for you? How does, or might, it help you to pay attention?
- What is your understanding of the kingdom of God? For example, do you view it as an ideal for life on earth, as the dwelling place for all who die in Christ, or as a potential reality on earth (to offer only three ideas)? What connections do you see between the ministry of Christ, the kingdom of God, and the mission of your congregation?
- Reflect on one of Jesus' parables. Which of them most challenges, encourages, or baffles you?
- Compare your portrait of Jesus with the one the author sketched. What are the major similarities and contrasts?
- Reflect on where your congregation stores its "treasure," the quality of light shone by its "eye/lamp," and the God or gods that the congregation serves. If it is possible for the congregation to follow Jesus' teaching on these matters more fully, what might have to change in the congregation's life?
- Reflect on the discussion regarding anxiety and trusting God. Express your thoughts either on the author's comments or on one or more of the quoted sermons.

Chapter 4

Practicing Theology

Building a Frame for Congregational Attention

Theological reflection is one of the church's key practices for shaping attention, for helping us to know how and where to be present to loving God and loving neighbor. Theology guides us to particular places and topics in both scripture and in our world. Theology sorts and filters data. Theology frames what we see and lures us in one direction or another. Choosing a theological frame and living within it is one of the primary means that shapes our attention as Christians. Theology can and should serve as an everyday discipline, a framework and lens for seeing everyday life.

What if theology shaped a congregation's attention as thoroughly as Western understandings of the self and market logic function in our society? Certainly, that congregation would be better equipped than most to discern what God is doing in our world and what the fitting ways are for a congregation to join in God's activity.

But, to understate the case: theological reflection is not a much-beloved church practice in the United States. Anecdotes and survey research tell us that many folks, including many self-identified Christians, claim to be spiritual but not religious. When researchers unpack this statement, they find that people have a deep yearning for connection and wholeness (spirituality) but often choose to pursue that yearning without connection to particular institutions (such as congregations) and without disciplined practice.[1] Furthermore, many Christians often set spirituality in opposition to theology, understanding the former as appealing to heart and gut while the latter refers only to the head. The former is warm and real; the latter is a "head trip."

This false dichotomy bedevils us even in seminary education. A good number of students enter seminary with this split in mind, and three years, almost ninety semester hours of coursework, and numerous hours of worship, formation groups, and mentoring do not wholly overcome the rift. Some faculty members are adept at helping students develop wholistically; many, if not most, of us are not.

This dichotomy injures the church. Spiritual practice without theological reflection or any critical component may reflect a wind of the times that tosses to and fro, rather than the Holy Spirit's activity. Theology without other spiritual practices may also misshape a congregation, leaving it without the energy to enliven passion and compassion.

Practicing either spirituality or theology per se may sound daunting to some Christians. But I would wager that it is more difficult to convince congregants that the church should "practice theology" than it is to convince them that they should pray and read the Bible. Calling out the word *theology* in a crowded church will cause eyes to glaze over and mental grocery lists to start. A Protestant pastor will sometimes hear a congregant claim that theologians just confuse and complicate the Bible's message; simple application guided by prayer, sans fancy interpretation, is the ticket.

Well, I beg to differ. There is no biblical interpretation without theology. One cannot articulate the biblical message without first determining what the message is, or accepting what someone else has constructed. The contemporary church cannot apply the scriptures to its own context without judging what the biblical world was like, what the contemporary context is, and what the message is that we should hear and heed today. Furthermore, every time we bow or lift hands in prayer, we invoke an understanding of God. Every act of so-called spirituality is shaped, consciously or unconsciously, by theological understanding. Why should Christians pray to God in the name of the Trinity, or in the name of Jesus, or as Sophia, or with or without words? Why should we pray for our enemies rather than for their destruction—or vice versa, as the author of some psalms practiced (e.g., Psalm 137). Every act of interpretation, every prayer uses theology.

Theologian Douglas John Hall expresses well the church's need to practice theology.

> It may appear defensive and self-serving when a theologian asserts, in effect, that theology matters. But if by *theology* one means the continuous process of disciplined and prayerful *thought*

through which a community of faith seeks to understand what it believes and thus to be guided in its living out of that belief, . . . then to deny that theology matters . . . is tantamount to opening up the ever-ready floodgates of irrationality and mindless, boundless spiritualism. Worse still, it makes a gift of that spiritual energy to powers and principalities that have vested interests in deploying it.[2]

Hall expresses twin functions of theology for Christian community. Negatively, good theology will keep a community from mindless, thoughtless, irrational belief and practice, or even from colluding with evil. Positively, theology will direct a community's attention regarding who God is, where demonstrations of God's activity can be seen, and what God requires of God's people in particular times and places.

We Practice Theology in Congregations All the Time

If you believe in God as found in the Christian scriptures, then it is impossible not to function as a theologian, consciously or not. The Christian God is the creator of the universe, the author of love and justice, who is at work in the world. Every day, every nontrivial choice we make regarding how we treat others, the creation, and ourselves says something about our theology.

In this chapter, I hope to tease out some of the theology embedded in church practices. I want to take some everyday church practices, describe the activity in detail, think about the theology implied in these practices, and then imagine talking about those actions in a more explicitly theological way. Specifically, I will look at the offering, eating together, and conflict, in hopes of demonstrating that theological attention has some very practical consequences. Then I will suggest ways to strengthen the congregation's ability to reflect theologically.

The Offering

What Do We Do?

The preacher finishes the sermon. Either the preacher or the liturgist stands at the lectern and invites the congregation to join in prayer, that is, the pastoral prayer that often concludes with the Lord's Prayer. Then, the offering is introduced. The ushers march forward on cue. They will be dressed at least as well as the majority of attendees, often one level more formal in dress. They stand in front of the altar/chancel rail with silver-colored, wood, brass, or pewter plates. The plate bottoms are velvet-cushioned, which dulls the noise if someone drops coins in the plate and keeps them from sliding as the plates are passed from one worshiper to another. The ushers hold the plates in a receiving position as they bow for the prayer that initiates the offering. That prayer may consist of something simple, such as "All that we have, O Lord, we have from you. Bless us as we return to you from what you have give to us." The prayer may be much longer and contain phrases that remind the congregants of their responsibilities to tithe, for extending ministries of mercy through denominational appeals, or for continuing an ongoing local mission project. When the prayer ends, the ushers turn and begin the work of passing the plates down the pews, starting at the front and working their way back, until every person present (except, sometimes, the worship leaders) has an opportunity to put money into the plate. One or more musicians play or sing an offertory. Unless something in the music promotes the corners of mouths to turn up, you see few smiles.

Prior to the plates making their rounds, congregants reach into purses and wallets and pockets for checks, pledge envelopes, cash, or pocket change. If children are in worship, a parent will often give a child a coin to put into the plate. Some folks sit with eyes cast forward and little to no expression on their faces, arms folded tightly against their bodies. When the ushers have retrieved the plates from all the rows and the offertory ends, the doxology or other thanksgiving music begins and the ushers carry the plates forward. They hand the plates to the worship leaders who sometimes turn, walk toward the altar, and raise the plates overhead. This portion of the service concludes either when the worship leaders place the offerings on a communion table or altar, or when they hand the plates back to the ushers, who then take the plates to the church office where counters are ready to record the offering and to prepare the bank deposit.

What Do Our Actions Imply Theologically?

Money is one of the most controversial subjects to talk about in many congregations. One day, in a field education classroom at seminary, I tried to make the point that we can get emotional quickly about money. To illustrate, I asked the class to discuss the merits and liabilities of a pastor knowing how much people give. Within five minutes, students were arguing with such deep feeling that I needed to referee.

Ask yourselves:

• What is the state of the conversation about money in your congregation?

- Who is authorized to talk about money publicly, either in worship or in church business meetings?
- How often can you bring up the subject of money in worship without upsetting the majority of the congregation?
- Do you use the language of "offering," "tithes," "gifts," "stewardship," "collection"? And what does each term say about what we think the nature of our offering is?
- What is the connection between the offering and the sermon, both in terms of placement in the service (for instance, some congregations place the offering before the sermon) and in terms of what the sermon is and what the offering is?

Much too often, we act in church as if money is private and dirty—or, at least, antithetical to the ways of God. We split the material and the spiritual into two worlds, secular and sacred, world and church. Splitting the material from the spiritual distorts both and either denies or at least questions the doctrine of the incarnation—the Word made flesh. Clearly, in Jesus' teachings as well as in thoughts from Paul and the writers of the New Testament epistles, money per se is not ungodly. The author of 1 Timothy wrote that "the *love* of money is the root of all evil" (1 Tim. 6:10). Paul viewed so highly the offering he was collecting from around the empire for the church in Jerusalem that he risked imprisonment and death to collect and deliver that offering.

In each of these biblical examples, money as an end is a problem. If, as I have already asserted, we become that to which we attend, if we are shaped by our ends, then devotion to money as an end, as our god, will misshape us. For those of us in a consumer culture in which we emphasize earning or having money in order to increase our buying power, we often express our worship of money both through the number of hours we work and by the number of hours we shop.[3]

How Might We Think Theologically about the Offering?

Christians understand that life is a gift from God. We live in Christ; our lives are not, strictly speaking, our own. We *steward* them rather than *own* them. A significant part of life is energy, the sheer ability to do. As I mentioned in a previous chapter, in the book *Your Money or Your Life*, the authors assert that we "spend" our life energy in return for money.[4] Each dollar in our wallets represents some measurement of usage of the life God gives to us. To follow out this reasoning, I think this means that all of the money we earn represents our stewardship of life energy. All of the money we earn, not just a portion, belongs to the One who gives us the energy to "make" it.

Our use of money may be the most telling expression of the state of our spiritual lives. Our acquisition and spending patterns, as individuals and as congregations, demonstrate our priorities and habits. If we cannot acquire and spend except with the energy God gives us to live, then how we acquire and spend matters to our spiritual lives.

Money can be a powerful *means* by which to do good. Directed by spiritual ends, money is an expression of our spirituality. Therefore, when we receive the offering in church, we express and celebrate the energy God gives us to join in the good that God is doing in the world.

If we believed this, I suspect our offerings would be larger, our lives would seem less crowded and hurried, and there might be smiles as the ushers are passing the plates.

Eating Together

What Do We Do?

In her book *The Rituals of Dinner,*[5] cultural anthropologist Margaret Visser observes that we can interpret and understand a great deal about a culture by paying attention to how members of the culture eat. In many Middle Eastern traditional cultures, everyone eats from a common bowl, and family is often defined by who is permitted to eat from that dish. In a place such as the United States, if we are in a crowded fast-food restaurant where there are no empty tables but there are empty seats at some tables, most of us will not sit down and face a stranger—it feels too intimate. Yes, we can tell a great deal about a culture by observing how members eat, especially how they eat together.

Two of the primary "meals" Christian congregations share are the Lord's Supper (eucharist) and potlucks. Here, I will describe potlucks primarily and will relate them to the eucharist in the theological reflection section.

Congregants practice potlucking for a number of reasons. Sometimes, the only reason is to enjoy eating together. Sometimes it is done to celebrate some milestone within the congregation or as a way to welcome new members. At other times, leaders may schedule a potluck when initiating a program, such as a financial campaign or a neighborhood care program.

To prepare for the potluck, the janitor (sexton) or volunteers set up tables or chairs in the parish or fellowship hall, including a series of tables on which food can be placed for people to help themselves. The large coffee percolators are filled with water and grounds and plugged in. Tea drinkers appreciate the too-rare phenomenon of a hot-water pot that has not been "soiled" with coffee grounds (which always leave an unwelcome taste in the water). Depending on the time of the year and the region of the country, someone may prepare iced tea or lemonade.

Parishioners prepare dishes at home, either according to their choice or, sometimes, according to the course to which they have been assigned. They bring the dishes to church in modest containers or in more stylish dishes and carrying-cases made specifically for potlucks. When the foods arrive in the fellowship hall, someone attends to assembling courses: salads and vegetables; mini-sausages and egg rolls and other appetizers; main dishes from macaroni and cheese (both from a box and from scratch) to chicken to a famous TV-chef's meatloaf; desserts. Jell-O may be placed anywhere except for the main-dish table, depending on whether its contents are more salad-like or dessert-like.

Of course, it should be noted that some very large congregations now hire chefs or cater most of their common meals, and charge an attendance fee to cover costs. In these congregations, the majority of the adults in a household may work outside the home. Their time is a premium and they have enough discretionary cash to pay an additional food cost. They do not have the time or energy to put on a potluck of homemade foods. Nevertheless, even catered congregational meals represent a desire to eat together.

The meal itself opens with a prayer, often by the pastor. Either by a prescribed order of tables or in a more chaotic fashion, everyone passes by the buffet, carrying either plates and utensils from home or paper plates and plasticware provided by the church.

Seating arrangements are remarkable. Families may or may not sit together. Children often ask to sit with friends, sometimes at tables of their own. Adults may want to chat with church friends whom they do not see often enough. Singles may gravitate toward their own tables and form a "family unit." They also may be "adopted" by one or more couples or seniors, depending on the individual's age and situation in life. The same goes for widows and widowers. At potlucks, it seems wrong to eat alone.

What Do Our Actions Imply Theologically?

One could bet it would be difficult to find more than a smattering of persons who dislike potlucks. No, the food is not consistently good, or made of the highest-quality ingredients, but no one attends a potluck and compares the experience to multi-star restaurants! Rather, participants speak of the intrinsic value of eating together and of manifesting community.

Indeed, in congregations with multiple services and in which children and youth participate in church school while the adults worship, a potluck may be the most inclusive gathering in a congregation's life. People tend to notice and appreciate this manifestation of their community. There is something about eating together in a relatively diverse community that enlarges our sense of family and sensitizes us to an ethic that everyone should have food to eat.

At potlucks one often hears, perhaps more than any other comment, "There is so much food!" It is not unusual for someone to employ a biblical allusion to the Gospel stories of Jesus and the disciples feeding the multitudes with a few loaves and fishes. There is so much for this church family to eat.

What Might We Say Theologically about Eating Together?

Despite the allusions to loaves and fishes, however, how often do we connect potlucks with God's abundance, the Lord's Supper, the "give us our daily bread" petition in the Lord's Prayer, Jesus' meals with his disciples, or Jesus' references to the kingdom of God being like a banquet that includes a lot of unexpected guests at the tables? Reflecting theologically on potlucks will draw our attention toward gratitude, toward biblical stories of eating, and toward the unconventional character of life together in God's kingdom as we, the church, prepare to receive God's kingdom. First, a potluck could serve as an outward and visible sign of God's abundance. Again, how often does anyone walk away hungry from a potluck? Especially when we are willing to share with our neighbors, God's abundant gifting of the earth is evident in potlucks. Potlucks could help us attend to the God-provided abundance in life rather than scarcity, as our culture tends to condition us.

Second, the communal practice of eating together could remind us how extensive is the network of people on which we rely in order to have food at all: farmers, processors, distributors, truck drivers, store managers and clerks, buyers, and cooks. While we may want to debate this or that link in the chain, the network itself demonstrates our interdependency with other persons and with the rest of creation. Thus, potlucks could guide our attention toward the ways we depend upon persons and systems, as well as to the ways we could express our gratitude often.

Third, eating should remind us of the gift of daily bread, the petition in the Lord's Prayer for daily bread, of the many stories of Jesus eating with his disciples and with those persons with whom the good religious folks thought he should not eat, and of Jesus' use of banquets to describe the kingdom of God. The Lord's Prayer petition for daily bread follows the request for God to rule on earth as in heaven. Jesus' sharing table with outcasts is an expression of a kingdom ethic that does not exclude persons by categories (for instance, Samaritans, tax collectors, lepers). Banquet illustrations of the kingdom of God reveal that the kingdom is full of joy and celebration and that the rules by which we often live in our daily lives—rules about inclusion and exclusion, about who deserves mercy and what justice is—do not apply in the kingdom. Furthermore, the sacrament of communion is a foretaste of that heavenly banquet. We could view potlucks as extensions of the communion table. As such, a potluck should help us attend not only to having a good time with people we enjoy but also to welcoming those who are not like us, to share tables with all of God's invited guests.

Conflict

What Do We Do?

A cartoon I filed away pictures a clergyperson being fitted with a new robe and being told it is the latest in clergy fashion. The back of the robe sports a prominent bull's-eye.

When I speak with pastors and lay leaders regarding seminary education, one of the skills they think that seminary education should give more attention to developing is conflict management. Based on anecdotes from clergy, and on the number of books and articles on the subject of congregational conflict in recent years, it seems that conflict in congregations has risen in both volume and seriousness. Given the many challenges and changes facing existing congregations today, and the decisions that must be made when beginning new faith communities, the level of conflict is not surprising.[6]

What does your congregation fight about, and how does it fight? Do you fight more over issues or personalities, over the goods you want to pursue or the evils you wish to avoid? Do parties address each other directly or use phrases such as, "You know, some people apparently think . . ."? What does resolution look like? Does the content of conflict tend to include doctrine, practices, substantive issues, or seemingly trivial matters?

In your cultural context, when there is conflict, how do leaders behave? Do they ignore it until they cannot anymore? Do they choose their battles wisely? Do they remain relatively calm, nonanxious, and nondefensive when criticized? Do they try to be "nice" and thereby suffer the unintended consequence of dealing with a full-blown storm that, if they had confronted the problem in a timely and fitting way, would have been no more than a tempest in a teacup? Unless they have been trained in how to handle conflict well, most leaders—and followers—will engage in conflict as effectively as they do at home.

What Do Our Actions Imply Theologically?

Most church people, I would guess, think about conflict and church in a manner akin to how they think about money and church: they would rather that they did not have to mix. I have sometimes heard lay people, deeply disappointed that their congregation was suffering some brouhaha, say, "If I wanted to fight, I'd stay at work or even at home. I don't understand why we have to have conflict at church."

Behind such comments is an implied conception of what the church is. In theological terms, we refer to this as *ecclesiology*: theological reflection on the nature and purpose of the church. The implied conception of church when conflict arises may be that the church is supposed to be a harmonious community, a sort of fantasy notion of what a family should be. How often do you hear the phrase "the church is a family" and think that this should mean the church is a *harmonious* family—quite unlike the ones in which we actually grew up or currently live?

When Christians are in conflict with each other, what do you think God's response is? Do you think God is a father figure who desires peace "when he gets home"? Does God take sides? Or does God at times rejoice when the church is fighting about something that really matters?

How Might We Think Theologically about Conflict?

Whenever we consider the matter of conflict in Christian communities, we open links to questions about unity and diversity, harmony and discord, justice and reconciliation and peace. In other words, we raise questions and make assumptions about the very nature of the church—and about the nature of the human race itself.

Permit a few examples from the world of music. Does God intend for the human community to resemble a Gregorian chant, pure unison? Or is the intention that we live like a great symphony with God as conductor, lead musicians (spiritual leaders, exemplars) from whom each group of musicians takes its cues, all combining to play in multi-part harmony—but harmony still? Or should human community resemble a jazz band, with variations on a theme encouraged and dissonance both necessary and tolerated to an extent? You might see how attending through a theological framework congruent with one of these metaphors (for example, harmony) will result in a different way of seeing and responding to conflict than if you attended through one of the other frameworks (variations on a theme, with some measure of dissonance).

It is understandable that we do not want to suffer conflict at church. Many of us live high-stress lives, with endemically over-stimulated amygdalas (that center in the brain for fight-or-flight signals). Too often, when we see or are involved in conflict, we experience and observe hurt feelings, winners and losers, and anger. Who needs any of this anywhere, especially at church? So, it is understandable that we do not want to suffer conflict at church—but it is not reasonable. God made human beings finite. There are many consequences of our finitude. Two that relate directly to conflict are the communal nature of understanding and of sin. All individual understanding is partial. We each see from a particular vantage. In order to develop a more comprehensive understanding of any complex issue, we need multiple good minds. Good people with good minds and strong spiritual lives will still attend differently, see differently, and believe in different right courses of action! That is why the disciplines of conversation and argument are essential and learned (rather than "natural") practices for *any* community. Good communication skills, common reading, and strong spiritual lives can help us to conflict well. But conflict we will!

We also know that we will die. This knowing—or unconscious feeling—often leads us to grasp anxiously, to hold on to something, whether that is an individual and his youth or a congregation and its past. To the extent that we grasp anxiously, we separate ourselves from God and from each other. We participate in sin. Sin is not simply an immoral action. It is living a life in separation, at enmity with God and each other. Acting in sin and from sin leads to distorted attention and perception. Conflict will certainly result.

Given the inevitability of conflict in Christian communities, one wonders why it seems that so many congregants, and even leaders, act as if there should be no conflict in the church! God calls the church to resist evil, to seek justice, to live as disciples of one who conflicted with authorities and friends, and to live by a different set of rules and practices than societies often do.

Leaders would do well to acknowledge the inevitability of conflict by preparing well to deal with it. There are many excellent books on the subject, as well as skilled trainers—in addition to the New Testament itself. But we should not overlook the resource that an adequate theology of conflict could provide.

How Might a Congregation Develop Theological Attentiveness?

I suggest three ways.

First, pay attention to prayer. Theologians in the early church believed that a Christian could not think theologically without an adequate prayer life. Such would include not only praying often but becoming reflective about the content of your prayers—especially the prayers used in public worship and other congregational gatherings. Who is the God to whom you pray? How do you name God (for instance, Father, Mother, Rock of Salvation, Holy One, etc.)? Which attributes do you attach to God—gracious, all-powerful, loving, just? You also might try to write out some prayers and to reflect on them, especially the connection between prayer and your everyday activities. For example, for the church administration class I teach, I authored a prayer for each class session. In these prayers, I sought to integrate theology and the practice of ministry—since students at the outset of the course tend to think of theology as something separate from administration rather than the latter as a means of incarnating and practicing the former.[7]

LEARNING

Mindful God, font of wisdom and source of all that is true: you have endowed us mortals with brains and minds, with the capacity for knowledge and wisdom, with the awesome and sometimes awful abilities to adapt, to learn, and to change.

We know, however, that like the people in the wilderness, anxious in Moses' absence on the mountain, we pool our anxieties together, cast them into the fire, and worship the emergent golden god of The Way We Have Always Done Things. And we are not talking about "the church" alone here, as if we are not included. We, too, contribute to that false god. We, too, fail to trust in the future to which you lure us. We, too, at times can't learn the things that we should learn, and fail to cast out the things that preoccupy our attention. We, too, respond defensively rather than listen well. We, too, fail to learn and so fail as your disciples.

We ask not so much that you strengthen us as teachers as that you strength our capacity to be teachable. Make us mindful of Jesus, who is our teacher, and it is in his name that we pray.

STEWARDSHIP

Generous God, who wants nothing more than our hearts: you made us in your image. You fashioned a good and glorious world in which to live. You share your life with us. You give us your substance through all the means of grace. You call us and equip us to be partners with you in finishing the world and in mending the creation and the relationships that we have broken. We thank you for your unending generosity.

We must confess, however, that we have given our hearts away to many unholy treasures. We have gone and sold all we have not for the pearl of great price but for comfort and security and power and for the assurance that we are successful in the eyes of our culture that defines success as the capacity to consume.

Grant us your grace to refashion us as stewards rather than as owners, as a deeply grateful people rather than as an entitled people, as those who respond to your beauty with silence and with praise rather than with the drive to have and to consume, as a people with hearts of flesh and spirit rather than of stone.

In Jesus' name.

CONFLICT

Mysterious God, we know you through both testaments as a God of both/and: you are the one who makes weal and woe, and the God of shalom; you are the one who broke down the dividing wall of hostility and who, it is said, sent Jesus who sometimes divides before he can unite. God of mystery, we seek your will—and faithful people often hear differing answers regarding what you want us be and do.

We long for calm and harmony yet we have created a world full of storms and hostility. Give to us a spirit of discernment with which we can sort through our conflicts, learning from them the lessons that are necessary. Give us the courage to face conflict born of injustice and the energy to pluck up, to pull down, and to rebuild on a righteous foundation. Give to us spaces in our souls and our congregations where peace can make a home, and from that place of peace send us out, free from our blinding and numbing anxieties, to listen, to mend fences and to build bridges. Grant us the senses to feel evil when present and the power to resist evil in all its forms. When we must conflict, and intentionally or unintentionally, harm another, fortify us with a love strong enough to seek forgiveness. When we are so wronged, fortify us with a love strong enough to forgive.

We pray this in the name of Jesus.

A second means of strengthening theological attentiveness is asking a variation on what has become a popular question in so-called Christian culture: what did Jesus do? That is an excellent theological and ethical question. As I mentioned in chapter 3, that question leads us to study the Gospels. When asked often in the midst of deliberations in parish meetings, it would certainly fashion a theological means of attending to the congregation's world.

A third means of strengthening a congregation's ability to attend theologically is to read and study theology. As a Protestant who believes that two good minds will almost always decide better than one, I would much prefer to teach and preach and offer leadership in a theologically educated congregation than one in which theology, such as it is, is a trickle-down theology (from the clergy) or one that has not been tested by other than their own experience. As I mentioned at the beginning of this chapter, we are always employing a theological frame of reference, conscious or not. We cannot help but to make decisions regarding who God is and who we are. I think the church does well to become aware of how we are deciding, on an everyday basis, theologically. It also does well to learn to evaluate how fitting our theology is for the decisions we have to make.

What might studying theology in a congregation look like? The following section—a sort of interlude between this chapter and chapter five—is an expression of my imagination. I pictured a conversation between a pastor and four diverse parishioners. The subject of their conversation is a set of four different theological books, all intended to be read and taken seriously by the church. Could there actually be such a group in a local church that took theological texts, considered each seriously by asking what the text encouraged them to attend to? I certainly hope so. Please consider the following as a church-oriented theologian's version of *It's a Wonderful Life*!

Interlude

A Theological Conversation

To demonstrate the power of theology to shape a congregation's attention, I have created a four-month, four-book conversation within a fictional congregation. A group of four persons, with the help of their pastor, will wrestle with four theological texts. Each of the authors I selected wrote their texts for the church—with different understandings of scripture, of God, of what God calls the church to be and do. I invite you, the reader, to overhear participants' conversation and, as you are moved, to join in. There will be no concluding discussion questions for this chapter. Rather, I have distributed questions throughout each of the four book discussions.

What difference does theology make in shaping the church's attention? By the end of this fictional conversation, I hope you will join me in saying that it makes a great difference and will be encouraged to pay attention to the theologies with which your congregation attends. We, the church, should pay more attention to our theologies in use as we read the scripture and interpret what we see going on in our world.

Introduction: First Highland Church

First Highland Church, located in southeast suburban Metropolis and connected to the city historically by a well-used commuter train line, recently celebrated its 150th anniversary. The building that is its current home was built in 1957. The sanctuary features the laminated whalebone, upside-down ship's bow architecture that dominated Protestant Midwest church architecture in those years. The church "plant" includes the sanctuary, a fairly spacious fellowship hall in the basement, and a two-story education wing that, along with the basement classrooms, has never been quite adequate for the congregation's size. Membership peaked in the late 1960s at about 3,000. The decline to the present 1,600, with an average of 410 in worship, has been not quite steady. The biggest dip occurred in the last decade. When the church council hired a consultant to help them diagnose their situation, he concluded that low-energy leadership in the paid staff, endemically low giving levels, an underdeveloped adult education program, and the absence of any sort of public "signature program" to brand the congregation in the community all contributed to decline. The congregation's attention and resources were filled with a variety of fraying programs that wore well three decades ago. They were expending a great deal of energy on maintaining fellowship groups, worship forms, and structures that were long ago prepared to die. In addition, the congregation's culture has historically been that of a high-demand, low-investment congregation—meaning that laity demand much from the staff but little from themselves either in terms of church membership or in terms of discipleship.

An observer who knew Highland and attended a service twenty years ago and then returned today would note a few differences, besides more space between the congregants in the pews. Heads are grayer. Children and youth are fewer, although they are far from absent. While the municipalities surrounding Highland have all become home to burgeoning populations of Mexican and Central American immigrants, you will not see any of these ethnic groups in the congregation. There were no African-Americans in worship twenty years ago and very few in the community. Today there is a small population that has moved into Highland; some African Americans visited Highland Church, and a few have stayed. Another relatively new development is that the predominantly Anglo church hosts a Korean congregation of the same denomination. Ties between the congregations are cordial but not thick.

Pastor Betty Christopher, who was called to the congregation two years ago, knows that the congregation's direction must change under her watch. If the institution's path remains constant, despite the affluence of the community and the many resources available in this upper-middle-class suburb, within a decade the congregation will be selling its home to another congregation. Betty is a seasoned pastor, a fine organizer and administrator, a very respectable preacher, and—something the congregation has sorely lacked for about fifteen years—an energetic and competent teacher. While active in progressive issues in the denomination, she also engages respectfully and honestly with a wider range of persons and perspectives than 95 percent of her clergy colleagues.

Betty is also the sort of progressive for whom the words *church growth*, *evangelism*, *discipleship*, and *discipline* are not bad words. Historically, they are words—and practices—that Highland Church has largely avoided, however. Highland's membership is comprised of many teachers, corporate climbers, entrepreneurs, and small-business owners, all of whom exhibit strongly independent constitutions. "It is important to decide for yourself," "What I like about this church is that no one tells me what to believe," and "It is important to keep balance in your life, and religion should have its place but no more than its place" are statements spoken by some and believed by many. For Betty, theology matters. Theology orients attention and gives content to words such as *evangelism* and *discipleship*. She sees that the cultural Christianity of First Church, rooted in post–World War II national values mixed with middle-class personal morality, has taken it a long ways, but this value system no longer sustains the people. In fact, this value system may be a debt that could foreclose on the congregation's future.[1]

Pastor Betty has been casting seeds of change since she arrived, both within the congregation's official decision-making structures and outside of them. A prominent example of the latter is a small group she formed to vision with her. She refers to the four-person team as her Barometer. Each of the four is an influencer in the congregation, the people to whom, when they speak, members of their affiliated group listen. Each also lets Betty know what the "weather" is like in their group: when the sermon was dried out or rained on their spirits, what chilled or warmed them in the stewardship mailing, when a storm is brewing, and when it seems fitting to turn up the heat. [I created each of these four people hoping that you, the reader, will see someone you know, or even yourself, and will imaginatively join in the conversation.] The four members are:

- Stan Wachowski, a 78-year-old retired tool and die company owner. Stan's parents emigrated from Poland. He has been married for fifty-five years and is in good health. He has been a member of the congregation for just over fifty years. He is not a fan of change but he is always pragmatic; he knows that time passing means change. He is a reflective person, although he has never been much of a reader. He attends worship regularly, appreciates a well-ordered sermon, expects to sing hymns he knows (if he does not know one, he refuses to sing), does not tolerate anything that sounds like politics coming from the pulpit, and—even some fifteen years into his retirement—is still one of the largest contributors to the operating budget.

- Chad Stewart is a 22-year-old just-graduated marketing major who has managed to land that rare thing: a job in his field. With the help of a gift from his grandfather, he purchased a condo near the Highland train station. This location allows him to commute into the city for work. Like many others of his generation (the Millennials), he is civically minded. He participates in Habitat for Humanity's house-building projects and volunteers in his congressperson's office. At his college, several Christian groups were very active. Chad, who grew up in First Church, found a conservative group's coherent presentation of Christian orthodoxy to be compelling. While he still thinks he has an open mind, he is also highly critical of the way that First Church practices Christianity.

- Wanda Good is a newcomer to Highland and to the church. She is a freelance graphic artist with several clients who keep her busy in her home office. Along with her husband and their two middle-school-aged children, she is one of seven African American adults who have made First Church home. They chose First Church because it is the same denomination as the church they attended in their former community. The week after Wanda and her family first visited Highland Church, Pastor Betty came to Wanda's home. While they were hesitant to commit to a congregation with so few people of color and with such a different ethos from their previous church home, Pastor Betty persuaded them to stay. Since they joined, several of their African American acquaintances in the community have also attended and subsequently joined. Wanda is a deeply spiritual person who expects worship to be an uplifting and healing experience weekly.

- Geannie Pelosi is a fifty-ish, recently divorced mother of two grown children. She is a downtown attorney with a successful practice dealing with immigration cases. She speaks of her practice as a calling, the way she lives out her faith commitment in the world. At this stage of her life, Geannie expects church to be intellectually challenging, offering a variety of classes to feed her mind and her soul. She completed an extensive Bible study program at the church and immediately wanted to know what was next. She wishes she knew more about prayer and other spiritual disciplines. She is willing to invest far more energy and attention in growing as a Christian than the typical Highland congregant. Between the recent upheaval in her personal life and the chaos she faces in her work, she admires those rare persons who seem so focused and grounded. Pastor Betty is one of the people she admires.

First Meeting

The Barometer met together initially in order to get to know each other and to stake out their purpose. The meeting time was Saturday morning, from nine until noon, once a month. The group met in Betty's spacious office, spaced about a round oak table that comfortably seated the five of them. With what would become the signature coffee pot and pastry treats from a local bakery on the table, about midway through the session, Betty ventured, "I want to suggest that we read four books together over the next four months. The publishers categorize two books as church growth and the other two as theology. In fact, I think all four are theological, and the theological stance in each is linked to a plan of action. Theology grows out of practice and informs practice. I think it is time that this congregation develops a theologically informed mission statement that focuses our attention and guides our practices. I want us to feed our thinking by reading these four books. My hope is that we can function as a test group for using theologians to help this congregation to think theologically." She paused and checked the faces and body language. "Before I go further, I want to know what you think." Stan, his arms folded and his eyes cast down, replied first: "You know I am not much of a reader, especially of anything like theology. I've enjoyed several Bible studies in recent years and learned a lot from them. Why don't we just study more of the Bible together?"

Betty responded, "Sure, we could turn to the Bible to address any of our issues. But the Bible requires interpretation. Think of what you know about the Pentecostal church in town or about the Catholic parishes you've known. We read the same Gospels as they do, but why do we worship and participate in the Highland community so differently? One of the reasons is differing theologies. Most importantly, theology is talk about God, and we can't interpret what is going on in our world and respond well without having some clues regarding where to look for God's work. Another way to say these things is that theology gives us the language to know what we are seeing and hearing in the world. Do we see a wound or sin? Do we see a bleeding-heart liberal or grace and forgiveness? Do we see nature or creation? When we put money into the offering plate, are we funding the budget from our incomes or practicing stewardship as persons who own nothing? Do we see a happy coincidence or providence? Do we see a bum or a child of God? Practicing theology, framing our everyday experience theologically enables us to inhabit a world different from the one our everyday secular vocabulary allows us to see.

"Here's an example from within our own congregation. Stan, I've heard about the ministry council meeting that happened a few months before I arrived; you know which one I am referring to." Stan nodded. Betty continued, "It was highly contentious, wasn't it? From what I understand, the conflict as expressed in that meeting involved three groups. One was comprised of couples who had done Emmaus walks along with some of our folks who recently returned from a weekend church-growth workshop. They were using words like *evangelism, discipleship, cultural Christianity*, and the like. They were highly critical of the way the congregation carries on its ministry. A second group was our Habitat for Humanity volunteer team that had been pushing for the congregation to join with some other church groups to advocate for more affordable housing in our area. The third group seemed to think that the church was doing just fine as it is, that we should leave evangelism to 'Billy Graham types,' and that the church should stay out of political issues." Stan and Geannie, who were both present (and on different sides of the issue) at that meeting, confirmed Betty's account. "Well," Betty continued, "there were several very different understandings of what it means to be the church included in that meeting. I think it would be helpful if we could become more adept at using theological language, which is the church's language. Think about the difference between understanding the church as authorized to preach the gospel to the ends of the earth versus understanding it as equipping members as disciples of a kingdom that challenges injustice wherever it is found."

"Hold it," interrupted Chad. "Why do those two have to be in opposition?" "Good point," replied Betty. "They don't. In my theology, they must be wedded, as when the psalmist writes about justice and mercy kissing. I sharpened the difference in order to make the point. I would guess that, if I pushed the Emmaus group and the Habitat group to articulate their theological assumptions, they would be examples of the split in practice that we too often see in the church. The theology practiced by each group leads them to attend to the scriptures and to our context differently from each other."

Chad sat back, satisfied for the moment. Betty finished, "I am arguing three points in all of this. First, theology is much too important to be left only to the clergy! It is the church's language and the whole church ought to be better equipped to speak its native language. Second, theology focuses our attention. Where is God acting in the world? How do we understand what is going on, whether we refer to a church council meeting, deliberations at the United Nations, or debates about housing in this community? Theology is one of the primary frames that helps the church answer these questions. Third, we are enacting a theology all the time, whether we know it or not. Every time we sing a hymn, baptize a baby, pray at the start of a meeting, greet newcomers at the door, put money in the offering plate, eat Jell-O salads and macaroni at a potluck, open the Bible, or listen to a sermon we are doing theology."

Wanda, who had been smiling for some time, chimed in, "I know exactly what you are saying, Pastor. I've thought a lot about the differences between the congregations in which I was raised and this one. One of the big differences is that, in the suburbs, congregations sometimes decline to participate in the community and don't necessarily seek to minister to *bodies*. This was never an option for the congregations I've known. The needs in the city always include feeding the hungry, housing the homeless, holding politicians accountable to the promises they make. I guess city churches attend to their environment differently from the way First Highland does. The new thought for me is to consider the difference in terms of theology rather than simply culture and environment."

Chad agreed. "Yes, Wanda. I see that. I also see a difference between the kind of Christianity and Christian community we read about in college from what I experience here. Now, I know I have a lot to learn as a disciple of Jesus Christ. But I am appalled at how many people in this church practice Christianity as if being an American is more important than being a disciple. I swear, Betty, if you never mentioned the Trinity here and baptized without mentioning Father, Son, and Holy Spirit you would get less flack than if you suggested we ought to remove the American flag from the sanctuary—which would suit me just fine, by the way."

"Now, now," entered Stan, in a very fatherly tone, "I might be upset by both absences. And don't forget that among the freedoms that flag represents is the freedom to worship that some take too much for granted."

Betty, smiling like the Cheshire cat, intervened, "Excellent! You are helping me to make my point about how much theology influences how we attend, what we see, and what we think is right to do." Everyone chuckled and the atmosphere lightened. "I've chosen four books. I want to start with the most popular of the four, Rick Warren's *The Purpose-Driven Church*. Warren is a Southern Baptist pastor who has become extremely well known for his ministry with the unchurched. We'll follow with a theologian, Letty Russell, who wrote *Church in the Round*. German-born, she was a pastor in Harlem before joining a seminary faculty. Russell is a feminist theologian who has written extensively on partnership as God's standard for how women and men should relate to each other. Then we'll move to *The Empowerment Church* by Carlyle Fielding Stewart, the pastor of a very large African American United Methodist Church in suburban Detroit. Stewart, who earned a Ph.D. and decided to stay in parish ministry, will help us think about tradition, innovation, evangelism, and justice ministry all together. The last book, and the hardest of the lot to read, is Douglas John Hall's *The Cross in Our Context*. Hall is a Canadian theologian of the Reformed tradition who has written extensively on how to think theologically within North America, especially for an affluent church. He will challenge all of us, I think, to consider the connections between the cross, our suffering world, and what is the hope that only the church can offer."[2]

Book One: *The Purpose-Driven Church* by Rick Warren

Everyone had barely found their seats at the table in Betty's office and the first bagel was yet un-cream cheesed when Stan began, with obvious emotion in his voice, "I finished this book last week and I could hardly wait for this discussion to start. I can't remember reading anything in the last twenty-five years that both distressed me and excited me so much at the same time." All eyes fixed on him. It was clear he had their attention. "I am excited because so many of Warren's ideas are good. So much sounds so right—that the church is an organism, that growth is natural, that things grow naturally as long as there are no barriers, that a congregation should pay supreme attention to the Great Commandment and the Great Commission, that a church should be known by its sending capacity rather than its seating capacity. And, oh my, thinking about 5,000 members with each bringing their friends. All this is exciting to me, a whole lot more exciting that I usually get at my age." Chuckles and smiles abounded as he paused and then finished his statement. "But I have to say, I have never known the church he is talking about. I was raised Catholic and then converted when I married. I've never known a church that reached out, that emphasized ministry to the 'unsaved' or even used that language! And, one more thing and then I'll shut up, I feel very guilty thinking about how few neighbors, friends, and co-workers I ever invited to church. Frankly, I don't think I would know how. So, I feel excited and distressed."

Chad nodded. "I have similar feelings but for different reasons. I, too, was drawn to Warren's ideas that the church should grow and all that. But I also was uncomfortable with how often he talked about numbers and how little he talked about right doctrine. Now, I was a marketing major and I work in marketing, but I don't like how often he uses marketing concepts uncritically and with only thinly referencing the Great Commission to back up his concern for very large numbers. I admire his comment about judging a church by sending capacity rather than seating capacity and on the need to equip everyone for ministry, but it seems to me he spends most of his time reporting how the Saddleback congregation he founded learned to bring their target population—what he nicknames Saddleback Sam—in the door. Is this dumbed-down Christianity? And, before we're done today, I hope we can talk about his comment on the cross. Remember when he writes about keeping the sanctuary free of 'mysterious' symbols like flaming doves and chalices but then just glosses over the cross by claiming 'Everyone knows what the cross is . . .'[3] These statements really bothered me. I was wondering what the rest of you thought."

Pastor Betty waded in. "Both of you have made very important comments. I want to respond to several of them. Before I do, however, I want to give the others a chance to speak."

Wanda took the cue. "I really liked the book. The pastor of my previous congregation attended one of Warren's seminars at Saddleback in California. He came back preaching a lot about being purpose-driven. I think that is the heart of this book: being the church on purpose, living by biblical purposes, seeking conversion and growth in Christian living, paying attention to your mission, cutting away every distraction that would hinder you from that mission. I grew up hearing the language of the 'saved' and the 'unsaved,' that Christianity requires conversion, and that the church ought to reach out to bring others in. Every worship service included a time after the sermon when the preacher would 'open the doors of the church' and invite commitments to Christ and to the congregation. So, I have no problems with what Warren writes about growth. A healthy church ought to grow in numbers and maturity. The only quibble I have with Warren's writing is when he writes about 'liberation.' He uses the term to mean creating an 'informal, relaxed, and friendly atmosphere' in church. Please! Read Exodus or the history of black people in the United States and tell me you can stick with Warren's assumptions about liberation!"

Pastor Betty could not resist an "Amen."

Geannie then spoke. "Warren's book was a good read for me because I oscillated between cheering and booing! He stimulated me to think, to check my own assumptions, and to see if I could articulate my own position. For all of that, I am thankful. I'll put out on the table two thoughts he evoked in me about which I feel strongly. I was really attracted to one of his opening statements that God is making waves in the world and it is the church's job to find one of God's waves and to ride it. Based on the Bible studies I've done in the last few years, it seems that Warren is on very good footing here. God is at work, we should look for where God is at work and join in. My second strong thought is connected here, and it is a 'but.' But when has God's work been so popular that thousands flooded to join it? When I look around at the many problems in our community and nation today, I see a great deal of injustice and lack of compassion. Based on what I know about the God revealed in scripture, I am certain that God is making waves for justice and for compassion. But, they may be small waves! Small like the mustard seed. After doing the parables study last year, I could not believe it when Warren claimed that parables contain 'the unavoidable truth that God expects his church to grow.'[4] I think our congregation could and should do much more to grow the church. We don't talk much about evangelism, we don't know how to practice it, and we are not as great in welcoming the stranger and showing hospitality as we think we are. But Warren speaks of God's waves almost as if they are like rides at the new amusement park, that everyone wants to ride."

"Wow," responded Betty. "You've each said something really important for this congregation. Let me recount what I heard. Everyone appreciates this book. We received positively Warren's ideas about the church as organism, the importance of evangelism and growth, the need to be purpose-driven, the need to discern where God is active in the world and to join in, and the need to equip and send *disciples*—not only welcome and receive *members*. We have some disagreement about what growth means, what the relationship is between growth as numerical success and the gospel, and what the doctrinal foundation is for evangelism. And, while Wanda has experienced a congregation that knew something about how to welcome newcomers, I concur with Stan's judgment that Highland does not. Have I heard rightly?" All nodded. "Okay," Betty continued, "I want to ask us three questions that we should ask if we take Warren's theology seriously. The answer to each is connected to the others. And I think our discussion will revisit each of the comments you all have made. First, where do you see one of God's waves around us that we should ride? Second, remember that Saddleback determined to reach a particular target population, which they personified as Saddleback Sam. Well, if we designated a target, how would we describe our Highland Hal or Harriett? Third, the cross is the only Christian symbol that Warren explicitly designated as allowable in the place of worship, but he allowed it because 'everyone knows what it means.' Well, what is your understanding of the cross, and how does your understanding connect back to your answers about God's wave and a target population?"

Sam groaned good-naturedly and grumbled that such questions were hard work for Saturday morning. But, without delay, the group carried on a lively conversation that showed no signs of letting up when Betty interrupted at about 11:30 in order to draw it to a close. The group debated the merits of whether God was in the waves of spirituality seeking, of contemporary worship experiments (or traditional expressions, for that matter), of struggles in the national church regarding the meaning of ordination and of homosexuals and the church, of anti-war protest, and of new immigrant communities. They listened and talked about whether it is right for a congregation to identify specific target populations and explored how different those targets would be if they sought those who looked like themselves (as Warren suggests is essential), or focused on welcoming "others," or redefined what unites the current congregation with potential new members. Finally, they largely stuttered and stumbled when they spoke about the meaning of the cross. This surprised them, for each had participated in a goodly number of Lenten seasons and Good Fridays. But, after a few platitudes bubbled up, they could not think of much else to say. They concluded that Warren was wrong—everyone does not know what the cross is. Pastor Betty flagged that subject for the group as one they should come back to in the other studies, especially when they came to the final book.

"All right," said Betty. "If we were to compose a mission statement for our congregation guided by Warren's theology framing our context, what might it say?"

Book Two: *Church in the Round* by Letty Russell

The Barometer indicated the possibility of stormy weather as they gathered the second Saturday. Pastor Betty sent an e-mail reminder to the group the week before regarding the time. In response, two members, Stan and Geannie, hit "Reply to All." Here is a portion of what each wrote.

Stan: I'm doing my best to finish this book but I may not have completed it before next Saturday. Two reasons: first, this is the kind of book I have avoided my whole life. I am more of a doer than a thinker. I respect what Russell is doing—mostly, and as I understand her. But she is deep, and she is writing about a lot of stuff that I've never thought about. And, well, as a white male who has helped to build the world she criticizes, I've had a difficult time staying with her.

Geannie: I can't wait for the conversation to start! I loved what Russell was doing. She has put into words many thoughts that I've had in part but which I could not have articulated. A church expressed through roundtables of connection, solidarity, and partnership. Her emphasis on the church being with the poor and on men and women, persons of different races, and different economic classes working with each other for the sake of God's mission in the world. Spirituality as connection—with God, with ourselves, with the tradition, with people at the margins. Wow! She envisions the church that I want to be a partner in helping to create.

Stan was the last to arrive at the church. After he took his seat, Betty offered a prayer of thanksgiving for the day, the coffee, and these people, then she sat back. Geannie reached forward, poured her first mug of coffee from the carafe, and said, "Well, Stan, I guess you and I received Russell's book very differently." Stan nodded with his eyes and responded, "Well, Geannie, I guess I am feeling my age. I think I have stretched as far as I can go without breaking. Warren's book challenged me to think about the Great Commission and evangelism and the lost and welcoming in ways that I had not experienced. That was hard. As you all know, I am a doer, and I try to show integrity between what I believe and what I do." Everyone in the congregation who knew Stan admired his integrity. "And I have tried to be a good Christian as I've understood that. I attend regularly, I tithe, I serve, I pray and read scripture, I was honest in business, and I have been a family man. But, first Warren shows me that I have not tried to reach out to the lost. Then I read Dr. Russell." Stan shook his head slowly, back and forth. "If I take her seriously, I am going to feel somewhat ashamed. To use her terms, this society has privileged me because I am white, male, and have means. But God, she says, privileges people at the margins of society, those who are pushed there. While Christ is found in the church, she maintains that Christ has a special relationship with the poor."

Chad interrupted. "But isn't that what the scriptures say? Jesus speaks more about economics and about justice and compassion for the outcast than he does about, well, family and sexuality and the like."

"Well," Stan mused, "I don't know whether that is true or not. It may be. But that is not what the church has taught me all these years. And if it is true, then what is the Good News for me? It seems that the sex, color, and class I represent have been the cause of much bad news, if I take Russell seriously and agree with what you say Jesus says, Chad. And, I'm not sure I can go there."

Betty was about to make a pastoral intervention when Geannie beat her to it. "Stan, you know I love you, as does almost everyone in this community, I think." Stan gave a sheepish smile and interjected, "Oh, my, that sounds like a big 'but' is coming." Geannie continued. "No 'but,' just an 'and.' We love you Stan, *and* I want to say something that is often hard for white men—and white women, for that matter—to hear. It is very important that we each take theology seriously, as Pastor Betty has said. In order to take theology seriously, we need to think about what a theological frame of reference would mean for each of us, *personally*. But, before any of us judges a text personally, we should go back to what Pastor Betty said about theologians taking the gospel message and trying to apply it to a *community in a context* today. That year-long Bible study I completed emphasized that the Gospels and most of the New Testament letters were written to specific communities. Consider what Rick Warren did. He moved to Southern California, focused on the Great Commandment and the Great Commission, built a church dedicated to reaching the unchurched, reflected on his experience, and wrote the book. Letty Russell sees the Bible as an immigrant from Germany, as a woman, as a Reformed theologian, yes—but also as one who served a church in Harlem. I'll bet that she has the East Harlem Christian Parish in mind as she writes, thinking, 'Will my theological reflections mean something there?'"

"Okay," said Stan. "I'm tracking. But I don't yet hear the point you are trying to make."

"Sorry to take so long," replied Geannie. "The point is that the Bible was not written with any of us *individually* in focus. And theologians, for the most part, don't write with a particular person in mind. Rather, both the biblical authors and contemporary theologians write to *communities*. If this is correct, then our question should not be first or primarily what this text means for *me* but what the text means for *us*. Meaning, Stan, that unless you define your community as white affluent men, you could and should be looking at the text from a different point of view than the one you expressed a few moments ago. I'm saying try looking at the text with our church community as the context rather than yourself at the center."

Betty then spoke. "Geannie, I really like what you've said. Let me add two things before I ask Wanda and Chad to wade in. First, it is very, very important for all of us to keep God in Christ, rather than ourselves, at the center of our attention. What Russell is saying, in part, is that, yes, affluent white men have benefited greatly from the way society is organized and that this privileging has caused them—collectively—to assume that they are the standard for what is good and right. As a group, white men should be moved from the center. But, for Christians, the only one who can occupy the center of attention, who can be the standard of good and right, is God as known through Jesus Christ. The mission of God in the world captures the heart of the church's attention because that mission is the heart of reality.

"The second comment is that I want us to consider how Russell draws our attention to Jesus differently from Warren's frame. She asks us to consider Christ's ministry with those cast by society to the margins. In her reading of the gospel, those at the margins are 'the lost' that Jesus came to save. She brings in lots of scripture to demonstrate how important the outcasts were to Jesus' ministry and concludes that we, the church, will find God's activity among the outcasts in our day. To use one of Warren's terms, God creates a wave with the outcasts that the church should ride. I think it is hard for white males, white females, and maybe even anyone with means to hear this message about God among the outcasts."

"That is where I am," said Wanda. "Certainly, as a woman of color in this society I have experienced being marginalized. I won't tell you all the stories I could of growing up in the city and the ways that schools I attended, or ads I saw on billboards and TV and movies, reminded me that black and white are not equal in this society. Almost everything portrayed white women and men as the norm and all the rest of us were, well, not quite right. I am sure this is one of the reasons why church is so important to African Americans; it is the one place in the week we heard the message that we, too, with our faces, were created in the image of God and were precious children for whom Christ died. I'll also confess that, as I read Russell, I realized how much I've been influenced in recent years by social class. My family and I have far more means than I had in my childhood family. I've moved into the upper middle class, like most folks who live in Highland. For me, the challenge from Russell is about being an American—by the world's standards, a wealthy American. Before reading Russell, I really liked what Warren had to say about reaching the lost. Well, I still like the language of 'the lost.' But, if I consider Christ's work with those on the margins, from the perspective of a wealthy American, I am not on the margins. Those who are 'lost' to this society are. But I am also beginning to wonder whether 'the lost' might include those of us captivated by our material wealth."

After a thoughtful collective pause, Chad entered the discussion. "Well, I have been wondering about Russell's central conviction concerning what the church is: 'a community of Christians, bought with a price, where everyone is welcome.'[5] I want to think further about her claim 'where everyone is welcome.' I want to make two comments about that. First, I see a contrast between Russell and Warren on this point. Warren thinks strategically: we can't reach out to everyone equally all at once. A particular congregation will reach out best to those who are like them. Therefore, a congregation should spend its resources strategically by reaching out to a like population. Russell's ideal of church includes persons of different races and classes, as well as an equal partnership of women and men—I don't think Warren addresses this latter issue of gender equality at all. Now, I think Warren is right that no one congregation can reach out, or welcome, everyone all the same and all well. But I think Russell is right that the church is not like a club that seeks out and lets in only people 'like us.' So I guess there has to be something that draws us together that transcends appearances. This is why I think right doctrine, combined with right action, is so important. As Paul writes in Galatians, all of us have been baptized into Christ, which gives us an identity that transcends all of our other identities—race, gender, and the like. So, I can see that a congregation's theological commitments, expressed in action, make a tremendous difference regarding how and to whom we reach out.

"My second comment is related. I really liked Russell's emphasis on hospitality. In one of my college classes, we read Henri Nouwen's book on hospitality, to which she refers.[6] Nouwen writes that hospitality is making room in your life for that which is not you without requiring that it become like you. That is really profound. What would living like this mean for our congregation, or for any of us, for that matter? And, if I might, I think my generation has something to teach here. I know lots of people in college who come from racially or ethnically mixed homes: black and Asian, black and white, white and Asian, Anglo and Hispanic, and so on. We see lots of pressure in the media for public figures to choose one identity over another. Some of my friends with mixed parentage find themselves having to practice hospitality within themselves, and they are learning that there is a humanity that embraces multiple identities. And, as a Christian, I would still claim that our baptismal identity transcends all the others that our society offers or imposes."

Betty took a deep breath. "Okay, let's see where we are. We have all noticed that Russell calls our attention to the gospel differently from Warren's presentation, and we're wrestling with the different consequences that theology has for defining congregational faithfulness. The central concern for the poor and outcast in God's plan as revealed in Christ's ministry is one major locus of attention. A congregation's mission, strategically reaching out and showing hospitality to outcasts, is a second and related topic. A third is how we identify ourselves—to what extent do we understand ourselves, individually and as a community, by race, gender, class, generation, and as baptized disciples of Jesus Christ. A fourth is what is our understanding of the connection between right teaching or doctrine, right action, and a community which is able to welcome both persons who are not like them as well as to welcome that in ourselves which is 'other'? A fifth is an overarching concern: keeping God in Christ, and Christ's mission, at the center of our attention rather than placing ourselves at the center.

"Let me explain this last statement and who and what is at the center. I heard this concern expressed several times but especially in Stan's comments, in Geannie's response to Stan, and then in Wanda's additional comments regarding class and our position as wealthy Americans on the world stage. It is fair to say that we will most often act according to the interest of whomever or whatever is the center of our lives. When we hear the gospel, if we picture ourselves at the center, then our response will often be limited to actions that will keep ourselves at the center. If we envision God's mission at the center, and understand that Christ summons us to participate in that mission, then we are drawn into God's center. Theologians assist us to be ever vigilant or attentive lest the Christian church slip into idolatry, substituting our will for God's will and our interests for God's interests.

"So, if we were to compose a mission statement for our congregation based on Russell's theological perspective, what might it say?"

Book Three: *The Empowerment Church*
by Carlyle Fielding Stewart III

On this crisp, clear Saturday the Barometer was seated and ready to talk at 9:04. Chad was the last to arrive. He was easily forgiven because he brought the morning treats. The others especially appreciated his day's offering because, in the assortment of pastries he carried, he included each person's favorite. They knew Chad had paid attention to their preferences!

After Wanda prayed for the group, Chad was also the first person to speak. "Okay, now we have a book that *I* am excited about. It has its problems, but Pastor Stewart nails a number of the issues that I think our congregation needs to consider. I could not agree more on his major points: the mainline church has lost and needs to recover the language of sin and salvation, along with the practices of spirituality, Bible reading, evangelism, and social involvement that is grounded in Christian spirituality. You all know that I grew up in this congregation. I attended worship and children's church, then Sunday school, then I was confirmed and was in and out of church during high school. Certainly, I know we say a corporate confession of sin at least once a month, as part of the communion ritual. But other than these occasions, and maybe Good Fridays, I can never recall any preacher or Sunday school teacher asking us if we had accepted Christ. I can't remember anyone talking about the lost, or what difference a converted life might make in the world. Well, when I hit college, the world hit me. I had a rough first year. I won't go into the details, but I was wounded and disillusioned and vulnerable. I am very thankful that the Spirit led me to pay attention to an e-mail I got one day, an invitation to hear a 'when life has you down . . .'-type speaker. The evening was sponsored by one of the church groups on campus. To make a longer story short, I went, I listened, I was invited to commit or recommit myself to Christ. I cried, I was prayed for, I felt a deep warmth and light overcome me, and I experienced a desire and an energy to be made new. I look upon that day as the start of my conversion experience. After that, I regularly went to Bible studies, theology discussion groups, campus worship, and participated in service projects during several term breaks. When I graduated, found a job, and decided to live back in Highland, I knew I wanted to participate again in the life of my home congregation because I hope that I can be a voice and a force for the kind of change from embarrassed Christian to emboldened Christian that Pastor Stewart described."

Remembering how Stan felt strained to his limits during the last conversation, Betty decided to provide some perspective in hope of giving him some time to absorb Chad's statement. "Thank you so much, Chad, both for the pastries and for getting us started. I appreciated hearing a bit more of your story than I had known previously. I want to make two responses. First, I want to put a historical frame around your comments. Then, I want to dig a little more into Stewart's call for the church to use its language.

"The historical frame: in the nineteenth century, some church leaders and theologians debated whether Christianity had to include a conversion experience or whether one could become a Christian through being nurtured as a Christian. Theologian Horace Bushnell argued the latter point. He hoped that a child could be raised in such a way that she never thought of herself as other than a Christian. Obviously, this stance rubbed Baptists and Wesleyans and many others the wrong way. The opposing groups understood conversion to be an essential experience in the Christian life, a complete worldview, in fact. In this worldview, everyone is born into sin, everyone falls short of the glory of God, everyone needs to repent and believe, everyone needs to be saved. Nurture alone will not bring about salvation. Church actions follow from this framework. Frequent revival services and seasons, calling sinners to repentance, altar calls, lots of attention to sin and to what we call the economy of salvation—all this follows from a conversion-centered way of understanding Christianity."

Betty paused for a moment. Chad nodded agreeingly. Stan's lips were pursed and his mouth angled slightly to the left. Wanda smiled knowingly and Geannie was attentive both to the conversation and to the last bite of her cruller. Betty continued, "You know how we've been talking in Barometer about living in post-Christian times. Bushnell's beliefs were deeply embedded in Christendom, in creating and sustaining a Christian society. While there is evidence to the contrary, I'd say a lot of the theology, catechism classes, and church school curriculum that the older ones amongst us here were raised on reflected Bushnell's approach. That meant a lot of talk about being good citizens, developing a good self-image, and a focus on nurturing. No, Chad, we did not talk much, if at all, about being sinners in need of salvation, let alone about evil in the church or the church's role in equipping us for spiritual warfare, as Stewart does.

"Now, let's look at what a difference our choice of church language makes when it comes to attending and to interpreting our context. If we use a language of nurture, then we are likely to attend to those practices focusing on growth. In nature, things grow when they have adequate space and nourishment, when the environment is right. We understand growth developmentally—there are stages of intellectual and moral and spiritual development. So we program church school to move children, youth, and adults along their natural progression of stages. But life in the church will look radically different if we start with the premise that we all need conversion, that we are all lost, that sin blinds us to our Creator and from seeing ourselves as made in God's image. Do we preach nurture or conversion? In church school, do we follow a curriculum organized according to developmental stages or one that provokes confrontations between the people God has called us to be and the people we are, or—to get personal as conversion-oriented Christianity must—to provoke a confrontation between the person God has called me to be and the person that I am? And think about the difference in motivation for doing evangelism. What is the motivation for inviting a person into Christian nurture versus inviting a lost person into a saving relationship with Christ? Can you see the very different ways that the language of nurture steers our attention versus the way that the language of conversion presents? And, of course, not only our attention is steered by a theology of nurture or a theology of conversion. Money, energy, time follow attention. Our choice of theology has real, practical, material effects on this congregation or any other. This very large, crucial discussion is behind Pastor Stewart's arguments in his book. He rejects the Christian nurture approach in favor of conversion."

When Betty finished speaking, the group sat in silence for a few moments. It was not an uncomfortable silence, as this hiatus may have seemed in their first book discussion. Then, after sipping from her freshly filled coffee cup, Wanda ventured, "Yes, Pastor Betty. It is becoming very clear to me that the theologies we enact have practical consequences. Dr. Stewart's book, coupled with the others and our conversations, have contributed to my skill in thinking theologically. I can see, for example, how Stewart's perspective stands at a sort of crossroad between Warren and Russell.

Stewart expresses affinities with Warren regarding growth and using Protestant evangelical language. But he also reaches deeper into the tradition than Warren does, with lots of talk about formation. On the other hand, Stewart speaks of social transformation and of reaching out to the lost more like Russell does—but I don't see the two of them ever sharing leadership in the same congregation! Stewart writes extensively about the role of the clergy as powerful spiritual leaders. Russell spends more of her time developing the concept of the roundtable church in which many people share leadership.

"But I want to open a new question. I was raised in the black church, in a congregation similar to the one Dr. Stewart describes. Clearly, and as Chad has already underscored, First Highland is rather unlike the congregation he serves. But so is the Highland community context, and that difference brings me to a question. Dr. Stewart writes passionately that the church should strive to be a spiritually empowering community center.[7] Well, the role of community center is one that the black church has played and still does in some communities. But in suburban, mostly non-black communities, I don't see the church trying for the same role. When I look around in our town and the surrounding villages I see a Buddhist meditation center, a Hindu temple, several long-standing synagogues, and three mosques under construction, then I think about all the conflict in our world today in which religion seems to play a prominent role—and a lot of time it does not seem that we Christians are the peacemakers. Given these realities, should we strive to be the community center? Can or should we think of a community with multiple centers? I know we've talked in here about Christian orthodoxy, we've considered Warren's understanding of 'the lost' and how Stewart emphasizes the church's need to reestablish theological talk about sin and salvation, but we have not yet considered other faiths. As we formulate a mission statement for our congregation, what kind of attention should we pay to our role vis-à-vis that of other faiths?"

Wanda's question began a new round of conversation, coffee brewing, and pinching up the last bits of pastries. Toward the end of the morning, Betty offered her by-now familiar summary and question. "Okay, if we were to take Stewart's theological perspective and attend to our context through it, what would we want to say in our mission statement?"

Book Four: *The Cross in Our Context* by Douglas John Hall

The first flurries of the season greeted Betty and the Barometer as they exited their beds on this final Saturday of their book-based theological conversations. Betty left for the church a few minutes earlier than usual.

She wanted to be certain that the coffee was ready when everyone arrived—and that it would be strong. She knew that Hall's book would stretch even her most intellectually curious Barometer members; she figured they could use an extra caffeine kick to jump-start the conversation. "Thank God that Hall writes very clearly, for a theologian," she thought, "and in a manner that an educated lay person might, with effort, be able to follow." Otherwise, Betty would not have chosen to use his book. She knew that Hall takes on a theme that is absent from most church-growth-oriented theology and is held in suspicion by some liberationist and many feminist theologians: the roles of the cross and of suffering in the Christian life. However, she resonated so highly with Hall's approach, and was herself convinced that his writing held great potential for First Highland's ministry, that she resolved to risk using it. Also, as the coffeemaker reached its climatic sputter that signaled an almost finished brew-cycle, she recalled the group's surprising, near-mute response to the question regarding the meaning of the cross that Rick Warren's book had prompted. Betty wondered what the group saw as they read Hall. She decided she would open with that question.

By a few minutes after nine, everyone had arrived, coats and hats were hung, and the weather was duly lamented. After Chad's opening prayer, Betty began. "Well, congratulations on surviving the last of our four theology books. Let's begin with Hall by reflecting out loud what you saw in the book that most attracted your attention."

Stan, who was very quiet during last month's discussion, spoke up first. "I must say this has been an extraordinary four months for me. Each month I read a book I would never have opened on my own. Each month, by the end of the book, I felt slightly dizzy—each book disoriented me in its own way! I can't say it has always been a pleasant experience. But I have tried to respond rather than react, as Geannie suggested during the Russell book, and keep our congregation's context in mind rather than you or me individually. So, in reading Hall, I've practiced reading him as a commentary on our context rather than as a critique of me as a Christian. Now, I still feel critiqued, and not without reason. But I have been better able to stick with him that I would have been a few months back.

"Of course, I was struck by the way he uses Martin Luther's distinction between the theology of glory and the theology of the cross within our North American context. I might even say that this distinction stunned me. It stunned me because I had not considered the extent to which my upbringing as an American had influenced my understanding of Christianity as deeply as it has. As an American who lived through the Depression and fought for my country in war, I have always believed in this country. I assumed that there would always be progress, driven by free enterprise and technology and a desire to spread a better way of life to more and more people. Yes, I assumed we would always triumph over all obstacles and enemies. Given Hall's understanding of the cross, I was intrigued to consider that my belief in triumph has distorted what the cross means—or, perhaps closer to what I think, has made the cross sort of incomprehensible, except that Jesus died there for our sins."

Geannie was the next to reflect. "Well, this was sort of a mind-blowing book for me. Two things stand out: first, that we should pay attention to attention, to suffering, and to church communities. Betty, you've been schooling us to understand theology as a language that shapes our attention, what we see, and what constitutes a fitting response. So, Hall's frequent invocation of attention caught me often. What should the church in North America pay attention to? Suffering. Not the church's suffering per se, not my suffering per se, but the suffering of those whom this society either has left behind or refuses to admit—the "lost" as Russell and Hall might say. Of course, this insight resonates deeply with me, given who most of my clients are. I particularly appreciate Hall's use of Simone Weil, the young French philosopher who connected love, attention, and suffering so powerfully; attention to the suffering of another is the substance of love.[8] Hall's conception of the church as a cruciform people is so different from the triumphant church that Warren offered as well as that which Stewart offered. The second topic that stands out for me, however, is something I think I disagree with. He writes that, in North America, probably only African American congregations are acquainted with the 'fiery trials' that might afflict a church that tries to live out of the way of the cross. Well, I think he overlooks numerous other non-Anglo immigrant Christians. Some of those congregations *have* experienced persecution here on this soil. But many, many others include members who suffered persecution on their native soils and are sorely aware of the connection between being a Christian and being a martyr or a witness. I think the problem here is that there are many cultural contexts in North America. I can see that Hall writes mainly for the powerful, but he need not diminish the range of those who have lived through fire."

Wanda nodded intently and spoke next. "Thanks for that last comment, Geannie. I concur that there are others in the U.S. who have suffered fiery trials, perhaps Native Americans being among the foremost examples. I want to reflect out loud a bit, though, on the difference between triumph and triumphalism, as he uses the term. I think I see what he is saying about a theology of glory that avoids suffering, that uses Christianity to justify uses of power that are anything but good news for the out-group.

But I would not want our congregation or any congregation to give up on triumphing, on overcoming. I think Dr. Stewart could be accused of triumphalism in the way Hall describes it. Early in the book, Hall takes a broad swipe at the church-growth movement as an expression of triumphalism.[9] Okay. But don't we want to triumph over our fears and over evil? Don't we want to triumph over hardship? Don't we want to triumph over sin and its effects in our lives? The black church I've known preaches and celebrates such triumphs. And we don't want to limit such triumphs to the black church, do we? The way I look at it, if we don't offer people someone or something at church that has power to help them overcome suffering, then why do we exist? Are we not in the business of offering hope? Maybe Hall allows the kind of triumph I am talking about but, if he does, it is overshadowed in my mind with his call to pay attention to the world's suffering. Of course we should. But we also have to remain focused on what it is that we can offer to that suffering world; and we should practice offering that to everyone who walks into the church."

Chad took his turn. "I want to keep pushing in the direction I think you're going, Wanda. Hall writes that the theology of the cross has always been a minority voice in church history. He quotes some theologian who also says something like 'this theology is not pretty.'[10] By extension, it would seem that a cruciform church would also fall into the 'not pretty' category. This leaves me wondering how a cruciform church does evangelism. What would attract anyone to a cruciform church? Those passages from Isaiah we read during Holy Week come to mind, about the unattractive, physically beaten, suffering servant. Now, the *mission* of a cruciform church seems clear. In our local context, there is plenty of suffering around us, especially among newer immigrant populations and among the elderly who cannot afford adequate health care and who often must leave their long-time homes. They can't afford property-tax increases and they are outliving their pension benefits. Also, given the affluence of our community, it is sad to see time-starved kids who yearn for loving attention but no one is home to give it to them. And, there is no question that our nation's presence in the world, especially in the Middle East, has caused immense suffering—and I say this regardless of what may have been if we had not gone to war. When our government simply invoked the language of crusade early in the drum-beating, we certainly conjured a triumphalistic cross image that was unhelpful. But, again, how does a cruciform church do evangelism?"

The conversation continued until close to the end of the morning, waxing and waning. Betty saw that the Barometer had become more confident in using theological language as their time had passed. She reflected silently on the changes she saw in each person. Stan's encounters with perspectives from evangelicalism to feminism to theology of the cross. Wanda's ability to claim the tradition in which she was raised and interpret and adapt it to her new context in Highland. Geannie's continual deepening of her sense of Christian vocation in the work she does. Chad's wrestling with the demands both of truth and of living in community. For a few moments, Betty's attention wandered from the conversation as she thought about how she could utilize these budding lay theologians to help move the congregation forward. Then, a quick glance at her watch convinced her she would need to pray and meditate on the subject later. There was time for only one more question.

"Okay, Highland's theologians-in-residence," she began. Although everyone giggled, no one mentally pushed the moniker away. "If we were to create a mission statement for this congregation based on Hall's theology, what might we say?"

Theology frames attention. As I wrote at the outset of chapter four, some theology is written by theologians, and these writings can help the church to think about its life. But I also noted that a great deal of a congregation's theology is expressed in its everyday activities and acts of worship. In fact, paying attention to Christian practices holds great hope for strengthening our ability to attend to God and to neighbor. I turn to this topic in the following chapter.

Chapter 5

Strengthening Attention, Changing Minds

Practices of an Attentive Congregation

"Do not be conformed to this world but be transformed by the renewing
of your minds, so that you may discern what is the will of God—
what is good and acceptable and perfect."

—Romans 12:2

This is one of my favorite verses of scripture. It reminds me of a truth that
brain scientists and social researchers both confirm: our environment
shapes us. Our behavior is not determined by environment alone, our
brains and minds are not shaped by exteriors alone, but the environment
and the events of our lives greatly influence how we develop, who we
think we are, and even the very pathways and cell connections in our
brains. We are conformed to (literally "formed with") our environment;
our minds significantly reflect aspects of our social landscape.

But the other truth in this scripture is that becoming a Christian involves a transformed mind, a mind shaped according to the mind of Christ
rather than according to human social convention. And the mind of Christ
is supposed to be found among groups of Christian believers, in the
ekklesia—a New Testament word referring to those "called out" from
society to form the church. Christian disciples are shaped not only by
family, group, tribe, or social forces or events. Christian disciples are to be
shaped in their relationship with Jesus Christ, and this relationship is
mediated largely, but not exclusively, through Christian practices. More
specifically, this relationship is mediated through Christian *ecclesial* practices, church practices. It is a very rare person indeed who prays well
alone but never sat in a company in prayer, who reads scripture well

alone without ever having sat in a house of interpreters, who beholds others and acts with loving attention without having received loving attention. We must pay attention to the practices of being church.

In this chapter, I will explore the importance for Christians to attend to our practices in order to strengthen our ability to attend to that which we ought to attend. After suggesting why I think scholars and church leaders are devoting so much time to practices at this point in history, and then defining what I mean by practices, I will turn attention to several "focal practices" that deserve our best attention.

The Importance of Practicing

There is a "basics" movement afoot among many, many reflective Christians in the United States. We see it demonstrated in dozens of books and seminary courses and, I suspect, in church newsletters, bulletins, and to some extent calendars and meeting spaces. I am tempted to call it a "back to basics" movement but the word *back* turns our faces in the wrong direction. While it is true that we are retrieving basics from previous times and sometimes from other traditions, "basics leaders" envision a church that looks substantially different from any in recent memory. Basics leaders look not to the late Protestant establishment with plans for its restoration; rather, they seek congregations fit for the mission context in which North American Christians find themselves today.

The key word in the basics movement is "practices." The central concept in the basics movement is that the church needs to retrieve, revive, reform, and imaginatively invent practices that will equip the people called out by God to become the people of God, that will enable the church to participate faithfully and effectively in God's mission in the world. Re-envisioned practices include worship, education, evangelism, mission, sabbath, calendaring, communicating, meeting, conflict management, conversing about emotionally charged issues, planning, nurturing and equipping for ministry, age-level programming, leadership development and education, marketing, scripture reading, prayer, retreats, hospitality, justice and mercy ministries—to name some but by no means all! Theologian Dorothy Bass's edited volume *Practicing Our Faith* set the tone for much of the renewed discussions and treatment of specific ecclesial practices.[1]

Now, you might look at this list and say, "Well, we do a lot of this stuff now." Granted, many congregations could claim acquaintance with many of these practices. But, as we will see below, the issue is how much attention and intentionality we bring to what we do. Packing a Sunday morning to make it resemble time-compressed workdays is one way to "prepare" for worship. Creating space and clearing a calendar in order to be attentive to the practice of worship is another. Discussing an issue, or fighting about it, in a committee meeting may be a common practice, but learning "best practices" skills of conversation and enjoying an argument among persons equipped with emotional intelligence skills is quite another practice. Reading scripture and praying at the opening of a church business session may be a common practice. Including a teaching session on prayer or how to read scripture attentively in preparation for the meeting's opening exercises represents a different-level quality of practice—and, I would argue along with authors who have explored practices, the potential for better-formed Christian disciples.

Why is this a fitting time for a basics movement focused on practices? There is a widespread belief across the spectrum of commentators on Christian life in the United States that the post–World War II forms and practices of church are no longer working. This argument has been expressed in several ways. The perspective expressed by Alban Institute founder Loren Mead in *The Once and Future Church* has been one of the most talked about in mainline church circles.[2] Briefly, the argument goes like this: the Christian church has lived through three historical periods, pre-Constantinian, Constantinian, post-Constantinian. In the church's first three centuries, Christianity was an illegal religion in the Roman Empire, the boundaries between church and society were clearly drawn, and mission was at the doorstep of the church. When Emperor Constantine decreed Christianity to be the Empire's religion in the early fourth century, the church's boundaries became coterminous with the Empire's boundaries: citizens and Christians within, barbarians and pagans or potential converts without. Mission was directed at converting the barbarians in far-off lands. These stances, with their attendant practices, held sway—despite the American disestablishment of religion—into the twentieth century.

For decades, however, a post-Constantinian context has been emerging. The boundary between church and society has been reconstituted, not as tightly as it was in the pre-Constantinian age when the Empire was simply hostile to the church, but with an awareness that being a good American and being a good Christian may pull us in different ways and that our host society is sometimes supportive and sometimes hostile to the church's aims. Anyone who has fought zoning boards that do not want the church to expand or rebuild, town councils that do not want the church to feed or house the homeless, INS authorities who come after a congregation that claims to offer "sanctuary" to an undocumented person, and angry neighbors who think peace vigils are unpatriotic has ears to hear! Consequently, we see reimagined practices of adult Christian initiation and teaching about the faith (led by Roman Catholics), intense and life-changing spiritual-life weekend retreats and programs (such as Emmaus and Chrysalis), worship forms drawing on ancient traditions (such as Taizé, or the recovery of Easter Vigils in some denominations) and contemporary technology, and revised and even well-used mission statements focusing on the congregation's calling in its place.

From Civil Religion to Missional Christians

By way of illustration, I wish to speak out of my personal experience. As I was growing up, there were more practices available more often to form me as a citizen of the United States than as a Christian, a citizen of the reign of God. Consequently, I believe I was better formed as an American than I was as a disciple of Jesus Christ. Let me explain.

From the earliest age, I can remember being taught by my parents, by my schools, by TV, and by almost everything else how to be a good, middle-class, educated American. In public schools, at the outset of each day, we rose from our desks, placed our hands over our hearts, and recited the Pledge of Allegiance, which we memorized in either kindergarten or the first grade. We were taught to show respect for the flag and the country for which it stands. Every Fourth of July, my family either toted our fold-up lawn chairs to the parade route and watched and scrambled to gather candy and gum tossed by float and convertible riders, or I participated in the church youth group's parade float (we did cause quite a stir one year when we featured group members shackled by paper chains and a banner quoting President Kennedy to the effect that one person's chains mean that no one is free). When we sat on the parade route, my parents schooled us to stand with hands over hearts and to act respectfully every single time a flag passed by—which the vast majority of our parade neighbors did as well. On the Fourth or the Sunday nearest, we sang patriotic hymns in church.

Such actions prepared me to participate in mainstream American civil religion. Some contemporary scholars define religion as a set of symbols and beliefs that orient people toward the Ultimate. A civil religion is that set of beliefs and symbols that expresses what a nation most cares about. In the United States, we might think of the following as expressions of civil religion: regarding the flag as a sacred object (when someone burns the flag, we call it a "desecration," which is the dirtying of a holy object); treating several of our holidays (for instance, Independence Day,

Thanksgiving Day, Memorial Day) as "holy days"; viewing a group of persons (the founding fathers, Lincoln, Martin Luther King Jr.) as saints; treating a few documents (such as the Constitution, Declaration of Independence, and Emancipation Proclamation) as sacred texts. Civil religion is not a formal faith, like Christianity or Islam. But it has real effects. Especially in times of perceived national threat, civil religion intensifies; the aims of the nation and the aims of God are joined.

In the public schools, we were taught the American civil religion. Teachers taught us citizenship rights and responsibilities, along with the nation's history as it was written for our generation: not yet sensitive to non-Anglo points of view, never critical of any use of power, silent regarding events such as the Middle Passage, the Trail of Tears, and World War II Japanese internment.

Citizenship lessons were also taught powerfully and practically through scouting. In Cub and Boy Scouts, in addition to learning to camp and to tie knots, I also learned to line up, to salute authority, and to practice self-control by engaging in endurance tests and even an "ordeal." I was inspired to strive for a set of citizenship virtues, expressed in the Scout Oath and the Scout Law: "On my honor I will do my best to do my duty to God and my country and to obey the Scout Law. To help other people at all times. To keep myself physically strong, mentally awake, and morally straight." The Scout Law states: "A Scout is trustworthy, loyal, helpful, friendly, courteous, kind, obedient, cheerful, thrifty, brave, clean, and reverend."[3]

In multiple settings, through many occasions and hours—for five days a week, nine months a year, plus some evenings, weekends, and holidays—I was formed through practice to be an American civil religionist. Over the last twenty years or so, especially since I completed seminary and began pastoring, I have been asking, "Did my church do as good a job raising me to be a Christian as my home and culture did raising me to be a American?" I don't think so. I do not think I was taught equally well or thoroughly to be a good, kingdom-oriented, Jesus-centered, spiritually rooted, compassionate Christian.

Certainly, in defense of my church, it did not have nearly as much time to shape my life as my parents, friends, scouting, TV, and school did. I attended Sunday school one hour per week, often without worship, until I could no longer stand it. When I was twelve, for a few months I attended the confirmation class taught by the pastor, again for one hour a week. We memorized the Ten Commandments, the Twenty-third Psalm, the Beatitudes, and the Apostles' Creed. I attended youth group throughout high school and became a group leader. During high school, my participation in church practices did thicken. We were permitted to plan two worship experiences per year, and I was usually involved in both. I attended many retreats, though I remember very little of their content. To this day, however, I know that it is important for Christians to withdraw from normal activities from time to time to engage together in extended reflection and prayer.

But, for the most part, my church formed me rather thinly as a Christian disciple. In fact, the church often adopted practices from the American civil religion. The American flag sat stage right in the chancel, which was the place of honor. We sang patriotic hymns on the Sundays closest to the national holy days. Despite turbulent times in the 1960s and early '70s, the preacher largely kept the nation's turmoil out of the pulpit (I know now that such was not the case in every other congregation). Coupled with a relatively weak adult education program, this meant that the Christian faith either remained silent or was coopted into the civil religion. Rather than forming me into a citizen of the kingdom of God, my local church helped me be a better citizen of the United States.

Well, in post-Christendom, twenty-first-century America, this conventional form of Christianity will not do. It has lost much of its appeal and most of its power—its power to transform minds according to the example of Christ, that is. Christian congregations seeking to prepare disciples to love God and neighbor according to Jesus' way need to pay close attention to the practices of discipleship. Practices are the building blocks of our lives. They shape who we are. As we shall see below, practices do literally shape and reshape our brains. Practices also strengthen our ability to attend to this rather than to that. In order to change who we are, we must change our practices. If we are to be an attentive church, we should attend to our practices.

Defining Practices

What is a practice? I will work up to a definition, considering several current uses of the word on the way. We use the same word, *practice*, to refer to training and rehearsing on the one hand and engaging in the activities of a profession on the other. In order to prepare for a baseball game or a music recital, we practice. To practice is to train, to condition, to perfect one's craft. Think of the baseball player who takes one hundred swings or fields two hundred ground balls a day in order to improve. To practice is also to rehearse, to act "as if" in order that, when we are on stage or the field "for the real thing," we will feel confident, focused, and well prepared. Rather than being distracted by the crowd, the audience, or other competitors, a well-practiced athlete or musician will be able to focus on what is important.

We also speak of practicing law, medicine, architecture, ministry, art, and a host of other professions. To practice in this sense does not exclude rehearsing and training. Indeed, for the sake of their craft and of the persons served, professionals ought always to be in a learning mode. But practicing a profession includes an additional element. When we practice a profession, we engage in fitting activities for the benefit of others. We practice these fitting activities seeking a form of excellence. There is a standard for professional practice; practitioners worthy of being called professionals seek to improve, if not perfect, the practices involved in their practice.

Another idea that is associated with practicing a profession is the idea that education for a profession is concerned not only with the transfer of knowledge, but with the *formation* of the professional as well. I want to use this idea that education in practices forms a person, fits persons for their professions. I offer examples from law school and from seminary.

Professional schools today are among the many places that speak of education as formation, not only as the transmission of cognitive knowledge. In the 1973 movie *The Paper Chase,* John Houseman as Professor Kingsfield spoke his famous line to first-year students: "You come in here with a skull full of mush and you leave thinking like a lawyer." The understanding that law school informs and forms a person to "think like a lawyer" was recently impressed on me when my daughter began her first year of law school. One of the "formation events" of the first week was a ritual. The chief justice of our state's supreme court lectured the group and then watched on as each student signed a covenant statement vowing to act from here on as a professional and not only as a student. The book in which the professionals-in-training recorded their signatures was a handsome, leather-bound volume filled with the signatures of past classes extending back to the school's founding. The message to the first-year students is that they have crossed a threshold: they are not only law school *students* but also *professionals-in-training*. They come in thinking of the law and themselves in one way; they are to leave thinking of themselves and the law in another. This is education as formation, not merely as the transmission of cognitive knowledge from the full pitcher (the teacher) to the empty pitcher (the student).

Education as formation is also a hot topic in seminary education. The ministry of the ordained is a calling, yes. God calls, a person responds—often with the help of Samuels and Hannahs who attune the person to hear and recognize God's voice (see 1 Samuel 1–3). The church confirms this calling when officials certify a person's call and ordain that person. But ordained ministry is also a profession, in that clergy should have something to profess (the gospel), there is a body of knowledge to be mastered (divinity), there is a public to be served (the church and the world), and there is a code of conduct (ethics) appropriate to the fiduciary responsibility of being invited into people's lives at some of their most intimate and vulnerable times. We may be born with the capacities (the room space, so to speak) to profess and to serve but not with the requisite abilities (the knowledge, the character strength, the attention, the will). The abilities must be formed. Seminaries exist to help church professionals-in-training to grow the abilities requisite to their calling. These abilities include not merely cognitive knowledge but such high-functioning skills as the abilities to know yourself, to reflect in practice, to practice emotional intelligence, to demonstrate spiritual depth and discernment, to be adept at interpersonal communication, and the like. No less than law school, and perhaps more so, seminary is a place of *formation*, not only *information*.

These two examples of professional formation focus our attention on the processes of formation per se. But practices are not limited to professional formation. On the contrary, and referring back to the example of being formed as a civil religionist and being formed as a Christian, practices are everyday activities. I could even speak of the ways I was formed into being a Peluso! The foods we ate, the timing of meals, the rhythm of weekends and vacations, our church-going habits (I was in charge of polishing everyone's shoes on Saturday night and lining them up at the back door)—these are but a few of the practices that formed me into Peluso ways of living.

Practices Defined

Given this discussion of practices as training and rehearsal, as constituent elements of a profession or community in which one is formed, practice may be defined as structured, purposeful activity that shapes the lives of the persons who engage them. More specifically, *Christian practices are structured, purposeful activities enacted by disciples-in-training in order that they might attend well to loving God and neighbor.* Alternatively, *Christian practices are the activities in which Christians engage to prepare to receive the reign of God in their lives and to invite others to do the same.* In either case, practices are the building blocks of the Christian life that provide capacity and strength to receive the transformed world God promises.

The diagram below illustrates the importance of practices for Christian communities. Christian practices should focus and strengthen our desire and ability to love God and neighbor. They also will strengthen our ability to become more mature Christian disciples, who then practice with more excellence.

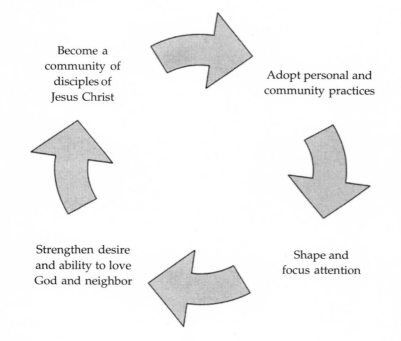

Become a community of disciples of Jesus Christ

Adopt personal and community practices

Strengthen desire and ability to love God and neighbor

Shape and focus attention

Diagram 1: The Importance of Practices for Christian Communities

Focal Practices and Focal Things

Albert Borgmann is a Christian philosopher who has given much thought to the importance of what he calls focal practices and focal things. He defines focal practices as those activities which center and illumine our lives.[4] As an example of focal practices using focal things, he invites the reader to consider the difference between a home centered around a stove and hearth and a home heated by a modern central furnace.[5] In the former type of home, many family activities happen around the hearth. Cooking, eating, reading, gathering for warmth and light—all these happen around the central source of heat and light. Now consider a home heated by a modern furnace, where these activities are scattered throughout the house.

Understand, neither Borgmann (who lives in Montana) nor I (who live in the Chicago area) are romancing the hearth and wish to abolish the advantages that modern heating devices represent. But with the shift from hearth to furnace came major changes in the way the family practiced being a family. The focal practices of preparing food, of eating, and of gathering for warmth and conversation around the stove/hearth (a focal thing) all changed with the advent of furnaces (an example of what Borgmann names "a device") placed in the basement or suspended from the attic rafters. Borgmann wants us to consider the changed or simply lost practices that accompany our technological gains and to ask which current practices might serve us well as focal practices and which things might be our focal things—practices and things that center and illumine our lives.

In the same way, ask yourself, Which church practices and things are or should be focal practices and things that center and illumine our lives, that enable us to attend well to loving God and neighbor, to receiving the reign of God and inviting others to do the same? In the following section, I will comment on three. Before I proceed to them, however, I want to consider how we practice. Engaging in designed focal practices requires mindful or attentive practice if we are to receive the full benefits of that practice.

Focal Ecclesial Practices

If we are to strengthen a congregation's ability to attend to God and to receive God's gifts, we will need to practice attentively. Recent brain research underscores the importance of attentive practice. As I mentioned in chapter 2, researchers tell us that our brains are capable of changing shape throughout our lives, a phenomenon scientists call neuroplasticity. When we practice attentively and repetitively, brain cells grow new connections (dendrites)—forming new pathways, cutting new grooves, in a manner of speaking. *Experiments indicate that activity done on purpose, with attention, can result in new learning paths; activity without attention will not.*[6] If we practice public worship or private prayer or church school inattentively, they will neither be the focal practices that they ought to be, nor will they contribute to being "transformed by the renewing of our minds."

But attentive practice may be different from what we think. Before I encountered educator Ellen Langer's writing on mindfulness and "the power of mindful learning,"[7] I thought mindfulness would mean what it often does in meditation practice: the practitioner seeks to sustain either a free mind or a mind focused on one thing. If the mind wanders, one brings it back to the focal point. Langer takes a more interesting and, from an educational viewpoint, practice-able approach. Mindful learning, as she uses the term, involves the learner's imagination: the learner takes the subject and finds as many facets or angles as one can. The focal subject remains central but the learner moves around the subject like an explorer who has found a half-buried treasure looks at the find from every possible angle. Consequently, in the following discussion of focal ecclesial practices, I will suggest ways that the practices could be approached mindfully and with more power to form us into the people God needs us to be. For example, when I worked with senior high youth, I led a Wednesday-evening Bible study at the parsonage. We concluded each evening with communion. One night, as we enjoyed the extra consecrated elements after the communion ritual formally ended, one of the girls said, "You know, every time that I eat bread and smell grape juice now, I am reminded of our communion services here at Bible study." I believe that she made the connections between eucharist and daily bread (a focal thing) because we celebrated eucharist frequently, talked of its significance often, and connected it with her senses of taste and of smell.

As this example indicates, we are sometimes shaped powerfully and unconsciously. And granted, not all important learning occurs consciously. But, as indicated in the above discussion regarding the importance of attending to practices today, it is a good time to attend mindfully to our practices, especially to those that establish as our focal practices. Engaging a focal practice mindfully or attentively will involve multiple facets, such as cognitive, relational, ritual, imaginative, sensual, and emotive. The more facets are engaged regularly, the more likely that mindful learning will result.

As noted above, the following practices are not the only focal practices for Christians. Others have written very well on many of them already.[8] The three practices I will comment on below include one that is written on extensively (worship) and two that are less extensively treated in the current literature (conversation and detachment). Each of these three is, I think, particularly important for relatively affluent North American congregations. They all have the potential to center and illumine our lives, to increase our desire to love God and neighbor, and to form us to receive the gift of the reign of God as we invite others to do the same. If practiced mindfully, attentively, they have the power to strengthen our ability to attend to what we ought and to decrease our desire to fill our attention with attractive distractions. Building strength in these practices would also help us counter the attractive distractions I wrote about in chapter 1: worship (technology, symptomatic conflict, preservation, size); conversation (reliance on technology and symptomatic conflict); and detachment (preservation).

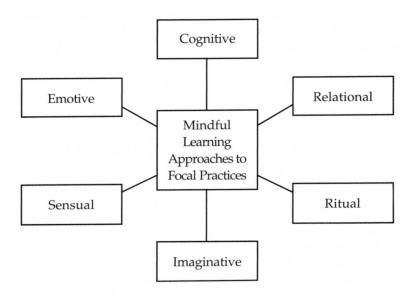

Diagram 2: Mindful Learning Approaches to Focal Practices

Worship

Worship is the irreplaceable hearth of the Christian life. It is the focal practice among focal practices. Paul Hanson is right: either we get worship correct, or we are mis-shaped as a people and our actions are distorted accordingly.[9] In his massive study of the meaning of community in the Bible, Hanson concludes that true biblical community is characterized by right worship which issues in righteous action. In worship, we take on the shape of the God we worship—remember, we become who and what we attend to.

To worship or to plan worship without accounting for its shaping power invites peril. Essayist Annie Dillard wrote about the lackadaisical attitude she observed around her in the pews while attending worship and mused that, if we realized the power with which we played, or at least believed the words we hear in worship, we would wear crash helmets and cry for mercy![10]

Well, whether or not you picture yourself in a crash helmet in your favorite pew, her point sticks: we should approach worship with thoughtful respect. I have worshiped in many, many congregations in my life. I can recall very few where I did not see or hear several of the following behaviors: grocery lists considered; ushers coffee klatching; lay or clergy readers stumbling over the texts; a congregation half-singing a new hymn; communion liturgies dripping with rich metaphors and references to powerful biblical stories read through with thoughtless speed because the sermon "went overtime"; no space for silence. Said differently, I often see worship that is a piece of our everyday lives: time compressed; filled with commercials and noise; presented in bites; eaten like fast food, with about as much lasting fulfillment.

Have you experienced worship in the following way? If you have, please tell the rest of us the path! The imaginative scenario I present here is not the only way to worship attentively. I offer it as an idea rather than as the model.

Imagine that among a worship team's chief aims are (1) to foster a cohort of parishioners who *attend* worship believing that their participation may change them, may transform them, may render them more capable of loving like Jesus loves and (2) to create worship events worthy of such expectations. What if the typical one-hour Anglo-culture Protestant service, or at least one of the Sunday morning services in a multiple service schedule, were stretched to ninety minutes? The first half hour could be used to teach, to warm up, as a liminal space. Liminal space is space that is betwixt and between. Ancient religious sites and buildings have spaces—gates, heavy doors guarded by gargoyles or other fearsome creatures, deserts to cross or mountains to climb—that set them off from ordinary space and time. Let's make the assumption that worshipers do not come to church prepared to worship but, after a liminal space and time, they could be.

In that liminal space, we could teach and acclimate the congregation to the morning's service, such as explaining the focal things (scriptures, hymns, prayers, water, and bread). This would add a cognitive dimension that might also invite ties to already-present emotive and ritual dimensions. We could introduce and practice a new hymn; tell the story that issued in a song; unpack the metaphors and references in the prayer of Great Thanksgiving; present some background on the biblical texts that did not make it into the sermon. Leaders could ask a provocative question related to the service's content and to something in the worshipers' lives, then ask them to write down their answers. This could be a time to create one or more visual centers specific to the service and call attention to them.

How would you prepare the congregation? What would you need to do in order to discourage attendees from thinking of the first half hour as optional? (For instance, one might start publicity and teaching moments three to six months in advance, generate conversation in adult church school and fellowship groups, prepare posters and other visuals.) What would you need to teach them about what worship is and how to approach worship? How might you use the congregation's present architecture to create a sense of transitional space as people move from their harried lives into the worship space? How could you use the senses of smell and sight more engagingly? How might you use emotion to express truth while avoiding artificial emotionalism? How would you work with a worship team to prepare such services? What would be the team's curriculum, their good learning problems? What would you need to read, where should you go to experience something of what you seek, what kind of commitments do you need from each other, in what ways do you need to be challenged to move out of your comfort zone for the sake of the whole people's opportunity to worship God?

Conversation

In the beginning God said, and things came into being, life came forth. Through the Word, John's Gospel tells us, everything was made (John 1). God speaks, and a matter is done or undone. God calls into existence and out of existence. It is as important for us to eat God's word as to eat daily bread (Matthew 4:4). Analogically, we human beings make worlds with our words. The first power God gave Adam to exercise was to name the animals God created from the earth. With our words we bring forth worlds of hate and violence, and with our words we heal, bring hope, and fill the world with love.

> A soft answer turns away wrath, but a harsh word stirs up anger. The tongue of the wise dispenses knowledge, but the mouths of fools pour forth folly. . . . A gentle tongue is a tree of life, but perverseness in it breaks the spirit. (Prov. 15:1-2, 4)

> It is not what goes into the mouth that defiles a person, but it is what comes out of the mouth that defiles. (Matt. 15:11)

> But Peter said, "I have no silver or gold, but what I have I give you; in the name of Jesus Christ of Nazareth, stand up and walk." And he took him up by the right hand and raised him up; and immediately his feet and ankles were made strong. (Acts 3:6-7)

> If we put bits into the mouths of horses to make them obey us, we guide their whole bodies. Or look at ships: though they are so

large that it takes strong winds to drive them, yet they are guided by a very small rudder wherever the will of the pilot directs. So also the tongue is a small member, yet it boasts of great exploits. How great a forest is set ablaze by a small fire! And the tongue is a fire. The tongue is placed among our members as a world of iniquity; it stains the whole body, sets on fire the cycle of nature, and is itself set on fire by hell. . . . no one can tame the tongue—a restless evil, full of deadly poison. With it we bless the Lord and Father, and with it we curse those who are made in the likeness of God. (James 3:3-6, 8-9)

With our words we express to others what we have attended to and what we want them to attend to. With our words we speak truly and build trust, or we utter lies and sow distrust and confusion.

Surely, attending to how we talk with one another is one of the Christian church's perpetual needs. In our time, it is also one of the sorest. If we judge the health of our ecclesial conversations by reports from denominational conventions or by observation of far too many local church meetings, the cynical view of words that permeates our society has shaped Christian speech. The quick sound bite aired a legion of times, the salacious lie repeated often enough until even legitimate news outlets report it as a factual account of what happened, lip-synching leaders who speak for a cabal of clandestine backers, the hands and tongues hired to spin every important event in the interest of someone other than the public good or of truth—these distorted message forms and messengers rule the day. Within the church, paying attention to winning and keeping power dominates our collective "cortical map" far more than attending to improving our capacity to listen or "to speak the truth with love." The ability to converse is God's gift to humankind. When we human beings disagree with one another, or feel fearful or angry, conversation is our main alternative to violence. When we do not pay attention to guard the veracity and kindness of our speech, however, we distort God's gift and turn words into a prelude to violence. When we can no longer trust the other's word, we will protect ourselves.

Theologian David Tracy has written that there is "no religious . . . tradition of interpretation that does not ultimately live by the quality of its conversation."[11] To converse is to turn together to view or re-view the world and then to ask about the world we should make together. What kind of world are we trying to make and mend with God? If creation is a gift, and God's new creation and kingdom is a gift, what do we need to do to receive it, to prepare ourselves, to set down in order that we have space and attention in our lives to devote to God's gifts? If God's nature is primarily compassion, hospitality, and love, then how should the church shape our codes of morality and purity? This is high-stakes conversation, deserving of high-quality attention and bringing our best selves to the table.

Good conversation requires focused attention. The focus determines the content of the conversation, and by means of conversation we attend together and, when necessary, change who and what we are attending to. A congregation needs to focus attention on God and on God's stuff. Now, this immediately involves a choice. God is a presence in absence, a mystery that is revealed and hidden. We know God through clues that the peek-a-boo God has left around for those with eyes to see and ears to hear. Which clues are God's clues and which lead to the wrong picture? How do we develop our abilities to see and to hear? If you believe that God is found especially with the poor, you may attend to different clues than those who commune with God on the golf course, or those who look for signs to join with God in cleansing the world of the weak and the impure. If you believe, with the Gospels, that weeds with tiny seeds and searching women and unclean persons are akin to the things of God, then you will attend to the world differently than if God resembles a cosmic action hero.

For Christians, it is imperative to learn how to converse. Conversation is a holy practice. It does not come "naturally"; there is nothing in the "old" (reptilian) parts of our brains to dispose us to listen well when we hear difficult words or to speak kindly when accused unfairly. Furthermore, the American people give little if any attention to models of good discourse. Rather, the "rhetoric" we hear from public figures on the campaign trail, in the halls of governance, and on the television may excite our amygdalas but far too seldom edifies or builds a foundation of truth and trust.

What if we *practiced* conversation at church rather than simply conversing inattentively? What if we treated conversation like dance? Yes, there are free-form dances, but one does not learn to waltz elegantly or salsa sexily without lessons and much practice. What if each month for a year every church meeting included a reminder on the holiness of conversation and a ten- to fifteen-minute focusing and practice session on how to talk with one another? What if a congregation trained a dozen people to serve as "conversation consultants" who would teach good practices and then be authorized to interrupt dialogue when less helpful patterns emerge and to engage the "teachable moment"? What if, on occasion, rather than allowing a few people to speak often while most are silent, or a couple of fast-talking extroverts dominating the pace of the conversation, meeting leaders encourage full group participation and move the conversation along at variable speeds by distributing a limited number of "talking chips" (one must be used each time someone speaks) or by passing a talking stick?

What are the *focal things* of conversation? The suggestions of talking chips or a talking stick are examples. We could also designate certain *tables* as focal things, holy places akin to communion tables and altars. A set of "table manners" posted on a wall and incorporated into opening exercises regularly might also focus attention. Dialogue partners in the ecumenical movement have developed an excellent set of such rules, through decades of practice, that translate easily in a congregational setting.[12]

In the final chapter of this book, I will suggest other resources that leaders could use to help examine such factors as the conversation participants' emotional intelligence, the congregation's culture of complaint and how commitments are expressed, and other cognitive and emotive factors related to conversation. Also, in the extended section that preceded this chapter, you will see another facet of attentive Christian conversation.

The Practice of Fasting from Consuming (Detachment)

In order to receive the reign of God in our lives, we need hands free to receive the gift. We need space and time and energy and attention to the practices of the kingdom. Those of us with full minds, crammed calendars, maxed-out credit cards and energy reserves, and tons of stuff to care for have no room to receive God's good gifts. We will need to detach, relinquish, let go.

Two observations: first, Americans have way too much stuff. Second, screens are everywhere—TV screens, computer screens, cell-phone picture screens—and much screen time is supported by a culture of consumption. Congregations would do well to promote fasts or sabbaths from consuming. Permit me to unpack these observations and judgments. Even if relatively few Christians in the United States practice fasting from food, I would wager that most know what a food fast is. And, given the state of Americans' weight and health, congregations would do well to promote and support fasting as a component of a healthy Christian lifestyle and of good stewardship. But I am arguing here for the importance of fasting from buying. I would like to see congregations support sabbaths from consuming.

A couple of the home-makeover shows on television feature homeowners living in chaos, drowning in their stuff. The show's host and consultants help them sort, toss, and rearrange stuff—mountains of stuff. Solutions almost always include lots of storage bins and "closet systems" (I do wonder how long folks keep up the new appearances). I have yet to hear a consultant say, "You know, look at how much stuff you are throwing out and giving away, and how much of that you purchased rather recently. The best solution to keeping your space tidy and your life manageable is to buy less. Spend less time shopping. Stop spending on that which does not satisfy or serve well."

Let's bring Jesus and Paul into the picture again with their teachings on things—teachings rooted in their own centuries-old tradition of practicing fasts, of abstinence, and of taking sabbaths from buying and consuming. One Sunday, as I sang in worship the stanzas from the hymn "Hope of the World," and the themes of this chapter were in my background attention, the following verse stood out: "Save us thy people from consuming passion by which our own false hopes and aims are spent."[13] I doubt that theologian Georgia Harkness had Americans' consumption excesses in mind when she penned these lines (more likely, Japan's and Europe's rebuilding after the "passions" of World War II). But the juxtaposition of "consuming" with "passion" and "spent" leapt out at me. We need to surrender our consuming passions, for the sake of the world and of our souls.

What if a congregation engaged in three or more of the following activities for, perhaps, the four months leading up to Christmas, and then for two months afterwards? What effect might they have upon the spending and giving practices of the congregation, both as a congregation and as individual Christians?

- Study one or more readable books in order to gain some critical tools and perspectives with which to talk about money and consumption. Joanna Ciulla's *The Working Life* explores the connections between work, money, satisfaction, and shopping. Joseph Dominguez's and Vicki Robin's *Your Money or Your Life* examines how money functions in our lives.[14]
- Sponsor a retreat on gifts, gifting, and thanksgiving, centered on Paul's thought, "I have learned to be content in all things . . ." (Philippians 4:11).
- Train someone to reflect with the workers after the annual rummage sale (proceeds of which often support missions) regarding the society that generates this kind of excess.
- Invite the willing to covenant together to spend less for Christmas and to challenge and support one another in this oft-times

difficult endeavor (we tend to think that "a good Christmas" is related to how high or broad the present stacks under the tree are).

- Promote an intentional decision to abstain from shopping one or more days per week—often enough that the participants know they have given something up.
- Form a study committee to examine how the congregation's program practices express or contribute to a consumer-centered mentality, which many—if not most—of us bring to church, having "spent ourselves" (poured out our souls?) during much of the week in our secular lives.
- Invite a denominational mission resource person to host an "alternative Christmas" fair, including giving gifts in loved ones' names to reputable agencies to reduce someone's suffering.
- Introduce gift making as a "focal practice."
- Promote and support "cleansing fasts" from screens. Abstaining from television, movie rentals, and Web surfing for as little as a week may prove difficult for most youth and, well, most adults. But a covenant group and a trained coach can be very helpful to participants when fasters discover the screaming void that is likely to surface when we remove the distracting practices.

So What?

Imagine a congregation where the leaders decided to attend mindfully to the practices of worship, of conversation, and of fasting from consumption. In writing this chapter, I thought I would pick three practices. Worship had to be on the list. Otherwise, I wanted to reflect on two more that had been long-standing personal interests. But, as I finish drafting this chapter, I find the three practices I selected fit together. We cannot serve God and mammon, Jesus declared. We cannot center our lives in consumption without being consumed by that demanding and stingy god. The stronger our ability to attend to God, the lesser the desire we have to serve a false god. I am not saying we won't be tempted. But at least we will recognize the temptations more often and will have the ability to choose whether or not to submit. Furthermore, we would be aided by an ability to speak well with each other. A well-developed ability for conversation, that includes speaking truthfully and lovingly and listening with truth and love, will increase our ability to attend to the signs of God in each other's lives and in the world around us. Through excellent conversation, reflecting on practices such as worship and fasting from consumption, we will grow in our ability to learn. We will also increase our receptivity to be transformed by the renewal of our minds.

The practices of becoming attentive to the reign of God in our midst involve hard work. We will not develop them casually. If a congregation is to grow in its ability to attend lovingly to God and neighbor, leaders will have to pay attention to what the congregation attends to and grow in their ability to frame the congregation's attention. In the final chapter, I suggest ways leaders might strengthen these abilities.

Conversation Starters

- Reflect on the practices that have formed you into a citizen of your country. Then compare the depth and breadth of those practices with the practices that have formed you into being a Christian.
- Which are your congregation's focal practices, the ones that most center and illumine your church life? What about focal things? What is your assessment of the strength of these practices and things? Consider the diagram on p. 104 regarding mindful learning approaches to practices. Might one or more of your practices be strengthened by working on an additional mindful learning approach?
- How would you assess the quality of the conversation within the decision-making life of the congregation? If there is room for improvement, which issue or practice should be addressed first? What would you be willing to do in order to improve the practice of conversation?
- What do you think about the statement, "In order to receive the reign of God in our lives, we need hands free to receive the gift"? If it is true at all, what might your congregation need to release, relinquish, or fast from in order to be free to receive God's gift? How about you, personally?

Chapter 6

Fostering a Culture of the Wise Virgins

Leadership in an Attentive Congregation

Seventy-two e-mails. Fourteen phone calls, not counting the telemarketers who ignore the "no call" list. Six people stop by, in addition to your scheduled appointments. The daily paper. The audio information and book service subscription. One hundred and forty-five satellite television station possibilities. The daily mail including correspondence, junk, solicitations, and subscriptions. Congregational reports. Denominational news. Conversations with family, friends, fellow congregants, acquaintances, and strangers. Meetings. Dozens of billboards and other ads at bus stops, on public transit cars and buses, popping up annoyingly and distracting you as you try to access the information you came for. The broken things and relationships from the past that you would like to fix but can't. Your to-do list. Your worries.

You deal with more "opportunities" to receive information in one day than was accessible in a lifetime to many generations, or is yet accessible today to many souls on our planet.

Now—in the midst of all this noise—attend to what matters. Harder yet, attend to the reign of God. And, maybe, harder yet again, help the congregation of multitasking, busy, distraction-tempted people you serve to attend to the reign of God like the wise virgins who kept watch, oil at hand and their wicks trimmed, always prepared to receive the reign (the bridegroom) when it appears.

The experience of being distracted is not new. John Wesley complained in the eighteenth century of the "dissipation" of attention, with so many amusements available then (!), which distracted the population from the reign of God. Lutheran theologian Joseph Sittler wrote passionately about the clergy's "vocational guilt" because the work they do in ministry often replaces the work they were called to do. He saved his most spirited words when imploring clergy to resist "the maceration of the minister":

> He, in his private and imperiled existence, must fight for whole-ness and depth and against erosion. *By a sheer effort of violent will he must seek to become his calling,* submit himself to be shaped in his life from the center outward. He need not be slapped into uncorrelated fragments of function; he need not become a weary and unstructured functionary of a vague, busy moralism; he need not see the visions and energies and focused loyalty of his calling run, shallowly like spilled water, down a multitude of slopes.[1]

How much the more is this true today than when Sittler penned these words in the late 1950s. Data streams, sound bites, and most information cannot save. Much of it cannot even help with the people and the problems about whom and which we care.

Building Key Capacities

In a powerfully distracting culture, leaders seeking to help a congregation be attentive to the reign of God face daunting challenges. Leaders cannot count on members walking in the door with roomy, strong capacities to attend. If a congregation wants to engage in long-range planning, often they have members trained in that skill. If a congregation needs to develop a Web site, often some member knows something about how to get started. If a congregation wants to hold a rummage sale, there are usually some people with demonstrated experience in those events. But it is not often that leaders can assume members' ability to attend with love to God and neighbor.

In order to attend with love to God and to neighbor, Christians need capacities (1) to enter with hope into suffering, (2) to practice emotional intelligence, (3) to engage the discipline of relinquishment, (4) to practice thankfulness in small things, (5) to "cook slowly," (6) to persist, and (7) to think theologically. How might we foster such capacities? The first way is to pay attention to them, beginning with yourself and the other members of your leadership team, which is what I am asking you to do now.

Capacity to Enter with Hope into Suffering

Attention is the most precious gift we have to give and that we can receive from another. It is difficult, however, at least in our culture, to be genuinely and fully attentive to suffering, either our own or others'. We seem to be born with a capacity for compassion, but our brains also dispose us to avoid pain and to seek pleasure. One could argue, in fact, that in the United States we built a culture around the denial of suffering. Our entertainment culture serves to distract us from massive global suffering, from the suffering in our neighbors, and from the suffering in our own lives.

The U.S. lifestyle is a shadow-side confirmation of Buddhism's first noble truth: life is suffering. Add together the cost of prescription (obtained legally or not) and over-the-counter painkillers, alcohol, "recreational" drug usage, and the various video screens through which we surf and at which we stare. The collective cost, surely in the hundreds of billions of dollars, testifies to our desire to avoid the truth that life is suffering.

H. Richard Niebuhr's famous line is a damningly accurate statement of the practiced theology for many congregations in the United States: "A God without wrath brought men without sin into a kingdom without judgment through the ministrations of a Christ without a cross."[2] Yet, the call to suffer is clearly at the heart of Christianity: "If any want to become my followers, let them deny themselves and take up their cross and follow me" (Matt. 16:24).

Please do not misunderstand. Christian suffering is not masochistic. The gospel does not call Christians to get up in the morning looking for pain. And taking up one's cross does not mean interpreting illness and disease and bodily suffering as crosses from God. Rather, to pick up a cross means to enter into the suffering of another. If Dietrich Bonhoeffer was right when he wrote that "only a suffering God can help" or that "when Christ calls [a person], he bids [that person] come and die," then it is likely that only a suffering church can help.[3] But as I tried to show above, our obsessions and anxieties, to the extent that they command our attention, hamper our capacity to be present to others in a helpful way. If a church cannot suffer with Christ, it fails its vocation. Clearly, God calls the church of Jesus Christ to live a cruciform life. A faithful church must seek to strengthen its members' capacity to suffer—with hope.

These last two words are essential. A strengthened ability to enter into suffering requires that we know the ground of our hope and that we know it deeply, in our bones. Thus, the capacity to enter suffering with hope means that our practices of theology, worship, prayer, and the like must penetrate into the crevices of our minds and the joints of our spirits.

Capacity to Practice Emotional Intelligence

Daniel Goleman, who has popularized modern brain research and its practical applications, writes about the amygdala, the almond-shaped part of our brain where the format of our early childhood traumas are stored. Later in life, when we see or smell or hear anything that resembles something from one of those traumatic incidents (the shape of a face, the smell of wood burning, a mannerism), the amygdala sets off the alarm system. Very importantly, the amygdala proffers us no sense of time: the time is always now. This means that, to the extent that signals from the amygdala control our actions, we will respond defensively—some form of fighting or fleeing—to many people and situations that are not really like the trauma.[4]

To practice emotional intelligence means to direct the so-called higher thought centers of the brain to engage our attention, to assess whether the threat is real or whether we have distorted present reality, and then to choose the most helpful and fitting response. To practice emotional intelligence means to think before speaking (rather than blurting out regrettable words), to own our feelings as our own (rather than holding others responsible for them), and to respond with equanimity to others (rather than taking emotional cues from them and reacting commensurate with their reaction). In Matthew's Gospel, Jesus contradicts the wisdom that we should take an eye for an eye or love only those who love us in return. His alternatives were to turn the other cheek and to love one's enemies also. He concludes this lesson with the words, "Be perfect, therefore, as your heavenly Father is perfect" (Matt. 5:38-48). While this scripture involves something more than a command to practice emotional intelligence, nevertheless, following this path requires emotional intelligence. Jesus illumines and commands a path of chosen, loving, attentive responses, in contrast to conventional reactions to insult and indignity. In order for a congregation to attend to suffering, with presence and hope, congregants must be able to practice emotional intelligence.

Anger often companions suffering. If you want to help those who suffer, you must learn to handle anger with emotional intelligence. My pastoral care professor in seminary told us one day, "If you cannot deal with anger, get out of the ministry." After twenty-six more years of living, and serving in three church institutions, I can testify amply to the truth of these words. And I can confess to my own continuing need to grow in emotional intelligence in situations marinated in anger, whether with a parishioner dealing with permanent paralysis after a stroke or with a group of seminary alums outraged about changes in their school.

Anyone who has ever participated in a church meeting either where something important was discussed or *should* have been discussed can imagine the benefit of practicing emotional intelligence. When important matters are at stake, anxiety is likely to be high, for anxiety expresses a sense of threat to our existence. Leadership expert Ron Heifitz, borrowing a term from the counselor's office, argues that when a group faces an adaptive challenge, leaders should create a "holding environment." A holding environment is a space, often figuratively speaking, in which a group holds on to its anxiety long enough to allow the symptoms to give way to the real issue, rather than spending attention and resources to bleed off the anxiety by treating symptoms.[5] In other words, a holding environment is a "safe space" in which the really dangerous stuff can emerge: that, based on its trajectory, the congregation will likely die within five years; that technology will not save the congregation from its ignorance about what the gospel is and how to bring it to itself or anyone else; that, metaphorically speaking, the congregation has spent itself preserving the frames (the building) while the paintings (the gospel tradition) have rotted; that disowning the pastor yet again will not change the angry, unforgiving disposition congregants exhibit to their leaders and to each other.

Any congregation would profit greatly from paying attention to strengthening emotional intelligence and the ability to respond with love, compassion, and unclouded judgment.

Capacity to Engage the Discipline of Relinquishment

Closely linked to emotional intelligence is the practice of letting go, of relinquishment. It is hard to be defensive and attentive at the same time. It is hard to treasure our obsessions and be present. It is hard to hook ourselves to our anxieties and to pay engaged attention to the person in front of us. We cannot serve God and mammon together. Neither can we embrace God's embrace of us when our arms are full of our mental and material *stuff*.

Here the church may be getting some help from our host cultures, for the language of "letting go" shows up a number of places. Self-help authors counsel readers to let go of destructive emotions, of obsessing over broken relationships, and of toxic current relationships. Influencers in the simplicity movement, whether through books or on various cable TV home and fashion makeover shows, advise readers and viewers to detach from their mounds of stuff (and occasionally, from the craving within that attracts the stuff). Moreover, relinquishment is not only advised but actually practiced in thousands of twelve-step groups, dealing with a panoply of addictions and cravings that beset humanity. The prayer often associated with Alcoholic's Anonymous includes thoughts on letting go. The full prayer, written by twentieth-century theologian Reinhold Niebuhr, is:

> God grant me the serenity to accept the things I cannot change, courage to change the things I can, and the wisdom to know the difference; living one day at a time, accepting hardship as the pathway to peace; taking, as he did, this sinful world as it is, not as I would have it; trusting that he will make all things right if I surrender to his will; that I may be reasonably happy in this life and supremely happy with him forever in the next. Amen.

Practicing relinquishment is also embedded in several of the steps themselves.

1. We admitted we were powerless over alcohol—that our lives had become unmanageable.
2. Came to believe that a Power greater than ourselves could restore us to sanity.
3. Made a decision to turn our will and our lives over to the care of God as we understood Him.
4. Made a searching and fearless moral inventory of ourselves.[6]

I wonder whether it might be effective to use something like the steps to identify attachments, obsessions, and anxieties and work at relinquishing them and their power over us.

As far as I can tell, no spiritual tradition in any of the world religions encourages adherents to accumulate stuff. On the contrary, each probes the dynamics of attachment and detachment and makes a virtue of the latter. Buddhism may be the most famous on this matter and has much to teach us in the West. But the Christian tradition is rich with reflections on letting go. Biblically, look no further than Adam and Eve leaving the garden, Abraham and Sarah leaving Ur, Moses and the people leaving Egypt, the psalmists writing during exile, Jesus' words to the rich young ruler, and the Last Supper. In the post-biblical tradition, writings from the desert mothers and fathers to Brother Lawrence, and from Teresa of Avila to Richard Foster, and many others provide a feast of experience with and teaching about relinquishment. Christian anthropology—what it means to be human before God as known through Christ—testifies to a sharp disagreement with our culture's norms of the acquisitive and consuming self. Christians in North America, especially those who have "made it" economically, would do well to cultivate the virtue of relinquishment, of letting go. In fact, cultivating and practicing that virtue may be one of the most important contributions that North American Christians could make to the world.

Capacity to Practice Thankfulness for Small Things

In North America, people of means often criticize those without for their entitlement attitudes. But no group demonstrates an entitlement mind-set more than the affluent. "Go ahead, you deserve it" is heard often in commercials, on talk shows, and is seen in books and magazines. All these present reality as if "the universe wants me" to be able to "celebrate life" with my five-dollar double mocha latte, or with pricey wines, or through a quarterly trip to the weekend spa. Those who can't afford such luxuries may feel deprived. But many who can afford these luxuries feel entitled to them. One of the largest problems with the entitlement mentality as it relates to affluence is that, as with those addicted to a drug that requires ever-higher dosages to achieve a high, there is never enough to satisfy. Entitlement, coupled with affluence, leads to the desire for bigger and for more, ever more.

But, in biblical and theological perspectives, we know that we were not made for affluence, for hoarding, and for consuming. We are not entitled. We were made for thankfulness.

At the core of the action of giving thanks is an understanding of what it means to be human. That is, to say thanks is to imply a particular understanding of the relationship that we human beings have to the world. That understanding conflicts with common values in our society, especially with attitudes of entitlement or self-sufficiency. At its core, to say thanks is to acknowledge that self-sufficiency is a fiction. Said differently, to say thanks is to witness to our connection to each other and our dependence upon God. To say thanks is to acknowledge that the acts of giving and of receiving are fundamental, essential acts of human life.

Perhaps the taproot of being a real, whole, healthy human being—an authentic human being—is to be able to give and to be able to receive. Either one by itself is insufficient. Those who cannot receive are diminished—for even God receives our thanks. No matter how strong a person claims to be, the person who is unable to receive is withered somewhere inside, like a branch detached from the tree. Those who cannot give are also greatly diminished. Like Mr. Scrooge, the miserly never have enough; it is unpleasant being around them. A complete human being is able to give and able to receive.

The Last Supper story is about receiving and giving and receiving. We refer to this last meal as the eucharist, thanksgiving. The actions of the eucharist may be the central actions of Christian living: take, give thanks, break, give, eat together.

Think about your day with these questions in mind:

What did I take and receive today?

- How about life? How about energy to do anything?
- How about breakfast?
- How about the pharmaceuticals that did not exist a decade ago?
- How about a piece of valuable information I did not have?
- How about a hug or a smile?

Who did I thank today?

- The maker of the alarm clock?
- The one who worries about keeping work on my desk?
- The one who fixed that tollbooth?
- The one who keeps traffic signals working?
- The one who delivered my paper, or mail, or food?

Think about everyone you depended on just to get out of bed (the bed manufacturer), to shower (rain- and water-table maker, well-digger, city workers, plumbers, fixture makers, gas or electric utilities, soap and towel and body and hair product makers), to get dressed, to eat breakfast, to commute—you get the picture. You could spend your whole day giving thanks for small things that, if you did not have, your day would fall somewhere between slightly off and miserable.

Then ask yourself, Did I take something I have received and break and give it like the communion loaf? Did I take something nourishing, did I take some of the wealth I have and pass it on, did I break off a portion of my time and energy to share with someone else? Did I allow myself to enter into someone else's brokenness in order that they would not be alone? Did I give someone who needed it my full and complete attention? Did I eat a meal with someone—not in front of the TV or a movie screen; was I present to the one who gives us food and to someone I love and eat with both of them?

What if we developed the habit or discipline or practice of giving thanks for small things? Giving thanks might fill up our whole day. Well, there are many worse ways to fill up our days—with obsessions and anxieties, with annoyances and pet peeves, with looking for offenses and finding the specks in our spouses' and neighbors' eyes.

In the media, we're encouraged to pay attention to very big things—the nastiest and most brutish acts of violence abroad or closer to home, charitable donations the size that Ted Turner or Bill Gates can give. But the gospel orients us to pay attention to the small things. Developing our capacity to attend to small things, with thanks, would have a salutary effect upon our ability to attend to the reign of God and to let go of some of the other stuff that holds us.

Capacity to Cook Slowly

While I was writing this book I found out that my cholesterol count was unacceptably high. The finding surprised me. Before I got this information, I thought I ate reasonably well. The doctor proposed medication, but I said I wanted to give myself three months on a low-fat, low-cholesterol diet to see what diet alone could do. This is the first time in my life that I have tried to diet. At the outset of this diet, I can confess three things. First, it is hard to stay focused and not to feed the cravings. Second, I found that I cheated my health with food more often than I thought I had. Third, I am the cook in the house, and it takes a lot more time to prepare healthy food than it does to eat poorly.

In North America, many of us literally buy into the culture that has turned food and eating into something akin to a device. Philosopher Albert Borgmann (see chapter 5) worries about the way that our unthinking marriage to technology marginalizes previously central events in life (such as food preparation). But, as with almost any trend in culture today, one can find a countertrend. In this case, that trend is the "slow food movement." The slow food movement began in Italy in the late 1980s and has since grown to over 60,000 members worldwide. Members desire to preserve food, family, friendship, rest, and hospitality from the acids of technologically driven, inhumanly fast culture.[7]

Congregations could strengthen their capacity to attend by practicing the institutional equivalent of the slow food movement: Healthy ingredients. People- (rather than technology-) intensive activity. A premium on savoring. Allowing the time that a dish needs. I am speaking metaphorically—but not completely! Speaking plainly: celebrate God's goodness with occasional feasts that revel in both the diversity of dishes and the complex makeup of each dish.

Can you imagine an immense difference, especially in congregations of predominantly Euro-American descent, between "slow food ecclesial life" and the much-too-common fast-food offering? Allowing the time to study and learn, to worship, to give meaningfully in service and mission—rather than gulping information bites and consuming just enough of the feel of worship to keep personal crises at bay a little longer?

It is disturbing that the connotation of "vital congregation" very often means very high activity, just like the rest of the members' lives at home, work, school, and in the civic community. I would like to see the definition of *vital* include persons and programs that are deeply attentive, that engage selectively and wholly, and that proceed at a deliberate pace.

As I mentioned in chapter 5, it might help to consider whether there is any way in a congregation's building to provide the equivalent of a transition space between the outside world and the inside. In some religions, a gate, a large and heavy door, or a passage creates a threshold demarcating sacred from profane space. For the most part, I disavow theology that divides the two, that creates a practical theology in which God is in the church but not the world. But, especially in many Protestant denominations, the "God is everywhere theology" (an attendant with the belief in a familiar, buddy-like God) has led to the ironic consequence that *no* place is holy. Marking a threshold into a church building might assist members to live into ecclesial time and space different from the rest of their lives. Such architectural space could also strengthen the practice of entering into worship as presented in chapter 5.

Capacity to Persist

Many ecumenical organizations, both at the state and regional levels, include public advocacy work. They track legislation, monitor city or state government as actions there affect the poor and the less powerful in our society. In studying these organizations over a decade ago, and subsequently having served as president of a state conference of churches, I became aware of one of those "duh" truths about which I was previously ignorant: things are as they are because someone wants them that way. A correlate is this: the interests that want things as they are count on churches and other civic groups to demonstrate short attention spans. Many church groups are notorious among powerful interests for creating brief bursts into the public realm and then quickly getting absorbed back into their less public concerns. In other words, the powers that be count on churches' impatience.

In my research, I encountered some very fine organizations that did not fit this generalization. These organizations engaged a public issue and "put their hands to the plow" only after counting the cost. And, once they did engage, they persevered.

A people committed to fast-food life and quick, leveraged results find persistence difficult. But can you imagine any significant problem, whether personal or ecclesial or global, that can be addressed well without persistence? School funding, teacher training, prison reform, corporate theft, publicly accountable government, refashioning our relationship with the environment for the sake of cleaner air and water and soil, transportation in urban areas, the habit of "spending" an hour a week and pocket change at church, racism and classism and sexism in the church, reclaiming the practices of prayer and of sabbath—making a positive difference in any of these requires persistence, readiness for the long haul. I'm told that an ox yoked to a plough will lean into the work all day, even if progress is slow. A horse will pull for a short time and will give up if there is no immediate progress. Real change work requires more oxen than horses.

How can we learn to hold attention to the same issue for a long time? With so many attractive distractions, and other good things that should be done always nearby, we are tempted to leave a difficult path prematurely. In chapter 5, I mentioned Ellen Langer, an educator who writes on mindfulness/attention and learning. She argues that mindfulness, or being attentive, in learning does not mean fixating on a single point from a single angle of vision. Rather, mindful learning involves focusing on the problem, yes, but from many angles of vision. In fact, the more angles of vision on a problem one can imagine, the better to hold our attention. This suggests that leaders might help congregations and denominations, where attention seems to be about as stable as a twisting kaleidoscope, persist in their work on a designated problem by regularly looking for a new angle of vision. In other words, try rotating the frame rather than moving on to a new problem with no dent made in the former one.[8]

Capacity to Think Theologically

This was addressed substantively in chapter 4 and the Theological Conversation. Here, I will simply reinforce two concepts.

First, theology is not a luxury in congregational life. It is an unavoidable necessity. But being a necessity is not the same as saying something is done thoughtfully. Much congregational theology is embedded in favorite hymns, in trustee policy regarding building use, in how baptism and eucharist are practiced, and in the messages sent to the congregation at stewardship time.[9] But learning to think theologically about everyday life—about living and dying, about meaningful work, about use of money and time, about school and civic community, about our government's participation on our behalf in world affairs, about forming relationships and breaking relationships—is an essential Christian skill. Congregants ought to expect that their called, elected, and appointed leaders will equip them to shape their attention theologically, toward the reign of God, and attune their resources accordingly.

Second, thinking theologically is hard work. "Seek simplicity, and distrust it," wrote philosopher Alfred North Whitehead. God is love. Human beings are made to give. These are simple Christian truths, but living them out in today's world is complex, arguably more complex than at any other time. Cultural anthropologist Clifford Geertz somewhere writes that we've created a world in which no one will ever leave anyone alone again—we are connected systemically through global market forces, in a common environment. Loving and giving in this world, interpreting who is my neighbor or how one demonstrates being a neighbor is often difficult. Douglas John Hall correctly writes that hard theological thinking means openness to suffering. To think hard theologically means to suffer—and to keep asking about and looking for signs of hope.[10]

Getting Started

For many congregations, the work of strengthening our capacity to attend as Christians involves adaptive learning challenges rather than technical ones. Recall Heifitz's distinction: technical challenges can be met within the current operational model, with the skills people already have. Adaptive challenges require a new mental model and new learning. Church growth and renewal authors do not often see "success" measured by a congregation's capacity to be fully attentive to suffering people.[11] Surely, defining success in this way, and living a life aligned with this measure of success, would be an adaptive challenge for many congregations—and for many of us personally.

No individual, acting alone, can "forge" an attentive congregation. Neither can a team of persons, for that matter. Through shock and awe, through the constant introduction of the novel or bizarre, and through generating compelling crisis scenarios, leaders can temporarily "grab" the attention of others. Grabbing is a far cry, however, from strengthening a people's ability to attend and helping them focus on what Christians should attend to. But a leadership team, such as I describe below, can covenant together to practice the disciplines themselves and to be yeast for attentiveness in the congregation.

Practically speaking, I suspect that on the one hand the outcomes of attentive practice would seem highly desirable for many people. On the other hand, as with diet and exercise plans, the rub is not in the end desired but in the changes in disposition and behavior that are required.

Christian attentiveness requires virtues that, as I suggested above, are little supported in our culture; in fact, together they may constitute an "alternative lifestyle." Gathering a team of persons, a covenant group, is a place to start the movement.

Leadership Team Covenant (sample)

In the presence of Christ and each other, I pledge to work together with team members to build bonds of mutual support and accountability. Specifically, I pledge to attend called meetings, do my homework, and pray for other team members; engage in the practice of relinquishment in order to strengthen my ability to attend; and seek with my team members to learn skills in helping groups converse, conflict, and deliberate together.

_____

Signature

Many congregations in recent years have instituted leadership teams either in addition to or alongside of official structures. Almost any congregation of any size could form a team of leaders, laity and clergy, who meet together regularly to support one another, to hold one another accountable for their discipleship, and to attend to the alignment and the gaps between the congregation's practices, its stated mission, and its desired vision. A team should include at least three people and probably not more than twelve. Everyone should be invested in the congregation's mission. Everyone should also have the abilities to address "big picture" issues, to work constructively with others, to hold confidences, and to risk. The activities I suggest below for a leadership team would require more time than a typical after-work evening meeting would allow.

If you, as a leadership team, sought to foster these virtues of an attentive congregation, how and where would you start? I would suggest the following work:

1. Foster the virtues of attentiveness within the leadership team;
2. Assess and address the gap between the current alignment of resources and an attentive alignment;
3. Identify and strengthen the congregation's focal practices;
4. Learn what it means for your congregation to do differently rather than to do more;
5. Strengthen the culture of thanksgiving and celebration;
6. Practice handling conflict well.

1. Fostering the Virtues of Attentiveness

In the three previous chapters, I argued that theology, personal spiritual disciplines, and congregational focal practices clarify what we should attend to: preparing to receive the reign of God. What can leaders do to strengthen these virtues of attentiveness—capacities to enter into suffering, to practice emotional intelligence, relinquishment, thankfulness in small things, slow cooking, persistence, thinking theologically?

First, pay attention to these virtues. Describe and record their presence and strength amongst your congregation as you begin. This description establishes a baseline. All these virtues are fundamentally relational and contextual; they do not exist in the abstract but are demonstrated in the way we live our lives in relationships and in our places. This means that the descriptions ought to include vignettes that illustrate how the virtues, or their opposites, actually work in your life. Here are some sample questions:

- When someone in my life is suffering, what are congregation's typical reactions, that is, do they want to fix it, do they want to make the suffering go away, do they want to put distance between them and the sufferer? In joys and concerns time, what kinds of concerns are raised? When we look at our mission statement, the committee and ministry team life of the congregation, what kinds of suffering do we pay attention to, and which types of suffering in our community and world do we tend to ignore?

- Based on how congregants behave at meetings, and especially how they behave when someone has caused a conflict or called one to a group's attention, how would you characterize the emotional intelligence of the congregation?

- What is the state of our teaching and practice regarding letting go of attachment to possessions, to the past, to wounds?

- What do we tend to say thank you for around here?

- As a congregation, do we tend to live with "time abundance" or "time scarcity"? Consider especially how we approach worship and fellowship meals.

- What are the longest-standing concerns of the congregation? When you reflect on that concern over time, what differences has leadership been able to make? Are there issues that you began to address and then dropped? If so, what happened?

- How would you characterize the theological perspectives present within the congregation? Look for clues by thinking about favorite hymns and about the aspects of worship, especially on Christmas Eve and Easter, that the pastor changes at her or his peril.

Second, each member makes a commitment to strengthen *one* of the virtues. As a start, one is plenty. Remember, this is a slow food, slow-cooking process. State your commitment something like this: "I am committed to strengthening my ability to practice *relinquishment*." You might consider doing this in the midst of a simple covenant service. Such might include forming a circle in which, one by one, the team members took turns stating their commitment, kneeling in the center of the circle, team members laying on hands, and then praying both for the person as well as for the group's ability to support and hold the person accountable for the commitment made.

Third, I highly recommend following the educational process lined out by Robert Kegan and Lisa Lahey in their book *How the Way We Talk Can Change the Way We Work*.[12] They ask a few deceptively simple questions that, in my experience, have never failed to dig deeply and helpfully:

- What are you currently doing or not doing that keeps you from fulfilling your stated commitment?
- If you think about stopping those activities, does anything like a worry or a fear arise in you?
- With that concern or fear in mind, what is the other commitment that you also hold, the one that exists in tension with your commitment to relinquish? Together, the two commitments and the tension that links them hold you where you currently are.
- Think about your hoped-for commitment as the heaven you desire and about the counter-commitment as the hell you want to prevent from coming. Then, ask yourself: if the hell that I am trying to prevent came into being, what is my assumption about my world and life?[13]

Permit me to illustrate from my own life. Relinquishment is a virtue I would like to strengthen. Every major world religion I know teaches the value of letting go, of non-attachment to all that rusts or dies. Jesus taught this virtue often, notably to the rich young ruler and throughout the Sermon on the Mount. Furthermore, hardly any virtue seems as important to me as a North American Christian than learning, and teaching, the value of relinquishment.

But what am I doing or not doing so that I fail to fulfill this commitment? Well, I have not systematically gone through all that I own and simplified my material life. In fact, in the last six months, there were more purchases, not all of which were necessities. Mentally, I have also not decluttered in any meaningful fashion—I still have as many interests, obsessions, anxieties, and "open loops" as I've had for some time. I have not taken on less to do. I have not relinquished hurts or jealousies. In short, while I can point to a few incidents where I practiced the commitment to relinquishment, for the most part, I have not. Why?

When I ask myself about the fear I have of letting go, I realize how thoroughly my sense of self is enmeshed with my stuff, both my mental and my material stuff. And I see that, if I gave away or sold my canoe and many of my books, I would have to acknowledge that I must close some doors at this point in my life. If I let go of the resentment I harbor against the few people in my life who have hurt me deeply, I might open myself to being hurt again. If I give up trying to please my family and friends in order that they will stay in relationship with me, what will become of those relationships? If I took very seriously Jesus' command to seek the reign of God first, do I really trust that all that I need for daily sustenance will be given?

These fears, then, represent what Kegan and Lahey call a counter-commitment. While I value the virtue of relinquishment, I also have a commitment to my stuff and my relationships, which all serve to define and express me. It is these two commitments together that create the tension for the current equilibrium in my life. Kegan and Lahey counsel us not to try to resolve a significant tension like this quickly because the knots, if attended to well, are opportunities for transformative learning.

A covenanted leadership team, dedicated to fostering a culture of challenge and support for each other and for the congregation in order to strengthen the virtues of attention, will be essential in becoming an attentive congregation.

2. Assessing and Addressing the Gap between the Current Alignment of Resources and an Attentive Alignment

Organizational consultants John Beck and Thomas Davenport argue that an organization's leaders must master two learning challenges: to manage their own attention; to manage the attention of the institution they serve.[14] In the previous section I addressed the first. Here I take up the second, managing the congregation's attention. Concretely, this work means stewarding the congregation's resources of time, energy, and money. No congregation can achieve a perfect attunement between its stated commitments and the expenditure of every dollar and hour and calorie. Congregational life is, or should be, too dynamic and human to be so lockstep organized and aligned. However, neither should a congregation's life be scattered and dissipated. In order for a congregation to fulfill its mission effectively and faithfully, there must be a "good enough" attunement between mission (which focuses attention) and the resources of time, energy, and money.

How might a leadership team assess the current alignment? I suggest a six-week audit and assessment.

- Ask the pastor(s) and the employed program staff to keep a time journal for one month, tracking how they spend their time (see the sample journal form on p. 130). Use categories suggested by the congregation's mission statement in order to organize the data, allowing that extra categories may be needed. Some mission statements tend to emphasize the new things a congregation wants to do, neglecting the maintenance activities that can consume all but a few hours a week. For example, a mission statement might read: "In response to Jesus' proclamation of the reign of God, Six Corners Church exists to invite people into Christian discipleship, to strengthen disciples' ability to attend with love to God and neighbor, and to send equipped disciples for ministry through the congregation and in everyday life." This statement suggests these categories: studying scripture and the "signs of the times" to look for glimpses of God's presence; evangelism and hospitality; disciple-building programs (such as worship, education, spiritual disciplines); and mission and ministry opportunities. It may be useful for each staff member, in coordination with the leadership team, to develop a daily log sheet that will include the date, the activity, the category or categories of work that they activity represents, the duration of the activity, and the level of engagement (see below). It is important to assure staff that congregational activities and not individual performance is what is being measured.

- Along with the time and activity journal, ask the staff to rank each activity according to the energy they were able to bring to the activity. In their book *The Power of Full Engagement*,[15] performance experts Jim Loehr and Tony Schwartz remind us that simply "putting in our time" is an inadequate way to go about our work. Both our satisfaction in what we do and our effectiveness is related to the energy we have to be fully engaged, fully attentive to the person or task at hand—or at least to be able to engage to the depth required. Rank each recorded activity from

Date	Activity	Mission Category	Duration	Level of Engagement
Sunday				
Monday				
Tuesday				
Wednesday				
Thursday				
Friday				
Saturday				

1 to 4: 1—very low energy, barely present; 2—low energy, present only by force of will; 3—good energy, enough to be adequately present; 4—very good energy, fully engaged.

- For one month of church meetings and ministry and mission activities, ask each person present to record their answers regarding the activity they engaged in and the level of energy engagement they brought.
- For one month of Sundays, ask each person who attends worship to answer one question and to offer an assessment before leaving the church: Which parts of the service, including particular songs or words or ideas or images, most powerfully drew you to them this morning? On a 1 to 4 scale [similar to the one I suggest above], describe the level of energy you brought into worship this morning, and the level of energy with which you are leaving.

At the end of the month, ask someone to compile and quantify the congregational data and the staff data. This data should provide a picture of what the church, as a congregation, is actually paying attention to, as well as the levels of energy or engagement involved. Then you are ready for two additional questions:

- *What is the relationship between your data and the congregation's vision for its ministry?* This question should get at how narrow or wide the gap is between what you do and what you hope you are doing. Using the above-stated mission statement as an example, how much time and attention did the core categories of the mission statement receive during the month? What level of engagement was staff able to bring?
- *What is the relationship between the congregation's expenditure of money and the data?* In order to address this question, it might be helpful to recategorize the money spent on employed staff from personnel expenses to program expenditures for ministry and mission categories. Again, it is important to emphasize that the congregation, and not individuals, is the subject of assessment.

What are the possible findings? You may find that you are happy with the alignment. Excellent. You may find that you are not completely happy but that the alignment is functional. Okay. And you may find that the misalignment is great enough to warrant some action and that the audit has helped you name a low-grade discomfort you've felt for some time. Perhaps you found conflicts and other energy sappers, although conflict well handled can also release or channel lots of positive energy. I would be surprised, given the stresses in North American life, if you did not find a lot of low-energy, tired people.

If you identified a gap between resources and attention that is uncomfortable enough that it requires your attention, what might be done to address the gap? The perspective I offer in the following four headings points toward an answer.

3. Identifying and Strengthening the Congregation's Focal Practices

In chapter 5, we met Albert Borgmann's concerns about our technologically saturated, device-driven culture, as well as his argument that we who live in this culture would do well to protect and enhance focal things and practices—the things, places, and patterns of action that focus and illumine our lives. In highly conflicted times such as ours are, congregations would do well to pay more attention to focal practices. The stronger our sense of center is, the fewer resources we are likely to spend either disputing or defending our boundaries.

What are, or should be, or could be a congregation's focal practices? As I argued in a previous chapter, worship, built on a pattern of word and sacrament, is the most important one. In worship, the congregation practices attending to God and receiving God's attention (that is, accepting the forgiveness of sins and living as a forgiven people). No work of the congregation is more important than the work of liturgy. This means that leaders must safeguard the resources necessary for excellence in worship, including the vital resources of all the worship leaders' time, energy, and attention. It is understandable and expected that, from time to time, the preacher will devote inadequate resources in preparing for worship. Too many funerals, critical illnesses, family crises. However, far too many congregations unknowingly conspire to keep their clergy and program staff on the verge of exhaustion for long periods of time. Too few congregants understand the resources necessary to create consistently high-quality worship. And, as Joseph Sittler, whom I quoted at the outset of this chapter, wrote, many clergy are shaped more by their congregants' driven lives than by the promise and responsibility of the pastoral vocation. If a congregation takes worship as a focal practice in the direction it should, leaders must expect that the allocation of staff resources is likely to change.

In addition to worship, other focal practices might include:

- *Annual dinners (pig roasts, ham suppers) and breakfasts*. I have heard that, in some of the faster-paced, affluent congregations, the kitchen areas in new buildings are smaller than they once were. There is neither the strength in numbers in women's groups, nor the desire, nor sufficient interest from men to maintain the kitchens of yesteryear. Such congregations may hire a caterer for both major events and for any weekly dinners. Now, I have no desire for congregations to continue stereotypical gender functions—*and* something is lost when the work of preparing our food is turned over to an outside party. In a rural congregation, the annual ham supper or pig roast involves literally the whole congregation—and sometimes more. It is a major intergenerational ritual constructed through practices of fellowship, mentoring, and hospitality. Such events are also vital fundraisers. Preparing meals used to be a focal practice. Now, too often, this activity is viewed merely as a chore. A congregation would do well to re-view and strengthen their practices of eating together, especially as an expression of slow food, gratefully received and eaten.

- *A process of growth into Christian maturity*. Here I am not talking about the orientation process per se (such as the opportunities for service, handing out boxes of offering envelopes), or the generic expectations many mainline congregations express regarding prayers, presence, gifts, and service. Rather, I am referring to the need, in a post-Christian culture, not only to orient but to disciple. Congregational leaders would do well to identify curricula for discipleship that is age- and ability-appropriate. Lay academies and certificate programs are steps in this direction.

- *Practicing emotional intelligence, contemplation, and meditation*. Other than strengthening the focal practice of worship, this may be the most important potential focal practice in a congregation's life. If the assertion is correct that our technology-driven, device-oriented culture has shaped our brains, and certainly has done nothing positive for our ability to attend, especially to attend to suffering, then we need to engage in practices designed deliberately to help us to attend. This work is difficult enough that, in order to practice attentiveness when it counts—in a meeting when the heat is rising, at home when your spouse has just pricked one of your defenses, in service when you're trying to minister to a dying person angry with God, in a congregation-sponsored forum on religion and politics—we will have to spend time strengthening our attention. Think of playing scales and practicing fingering in order to play music.

Buddhists and Hindus living in the United States and practicing their faith form the equivalent of Sunday school classes for the sake of teaching meditative practices that strengthen ability to attend. We Christians should do the same, for our own reasons. In the Sermon on the Mount, Jesus counsels his disciples not to react to the action someone else has done to you, but to choose a loving response (Matt. 5:38-48). Acting in this way requires emotional intelligence.

Christ calls the church to suffer with him in the world. Roman Catholic theologian Hans Küng wrote that Christ suffered alone on the cross in order to form a community in which no one has to suffer alone again. In order for the church to take up its cross, it must be free enough of the vampires of attention.[16]

- *The practices of filtering information and fasting from information.* In the absence of mental filters, we would drown in data. In this information-saturated, Internet-screen world, our individual filters buckle from the pressure and volume, like a submarine that dives too deep. Lutheran stewardship specialist Bob Sitze, in his book *Not Trying Too Hard*,[17] offers many good ways that a congregation can help its members filter information. His suggestions should be read as an attempt to help congregations (as well as the denominations and networks that resource them), using their values, to assume responsibility for filtering information, just as other institutions already have. It is very important to realize that filtering occurs within the context of a relationship. How can that be, since most of us do not personally know the people who decide what news we view on television, hear on radio, or see on the Web or in the newspaper? Most of us do not know the Yahoo or Google employees who decide whether the content of a Web page correlates sufficiently to be relevant to a particular search. Yet, it is highly likely that we, on some level, trust that the data they weave into meaningful information for us is fitting. We cannot filter and frame everything ourselves. Daily, and many times daily, we rely on others to frame and filter for us. Congregations ought to bolster their members in the work of filtering.

  One of the possibilities Sitze mentions is what I would call an information fast. In order to know how much attention practices like reading the newspaper, surfing the Net, or trying to find a worthwhile show on TV takes from you, encourage the congregation to abstain from the activity for a week or even a month. A fast provides the opportunity for a more detached relationship with our information sources. For example, for two summers, my wife and I abstained from television for a month. When we turned it back on, the commercial-saturated nature of the medium was bracingly clear to us. The fast made us more conscious and critical of both the form and content of the ads.

4. Doing Differently Rather than More

This phrase is a popular one in the business world. Managers pepper their speeches and e-mails with it, even as employees' multiple in-boxes overflow and cartoonists lambaste the contrast between the words and reality. Doing differently rather than more is much more easily said and wished for than done.

Central to my argument in these pages is that congregations, with their attention overwhelmed, scatter their resources of time, energy, and money. They often work to sustain obsessions and anxieties rather than to be present and attentive to receive the reign of God in the appetizers Christ offers regularly. We cannot take on one more thing unless we let something go. But, as Kegan and Lahey analyze our attempts to change, letting go of something is complex, for we work both to receive heaven (the commitments we publicly declare) as well as to prevent our visions of hell from coming (our defensive routines that prevent learning and change).[18] In the quest to become a more attentive congregation, leaders need to expect significant resistance to giving anything up because we either hold differing visions of heaven or fear that hell will arrive if we stop doing what we do in the way we do it—youth ministry, committee meetings, worship. And, without letting go of some current programs and practices and mental placeholders, a congregation cannot take up the work of strengthening attention.

The attention audit, which I described above, is one piece of doing differently. Another is developing the habit of asking three questions about new initiatives:

- Who has the attention to give to it?
- What resources will it require?
- Will someone need to let go of something else if we begin this?

Now, none of these questions is meant to stifle innovation or discourage members from engaging their callings and passions for ministry. But, if attention in people and groups is available in a fixed amount, then adding something to our attention requires us to give something up. Alternatively, of course, more people bringing additional resources expands the available attention. Members shifting attention from screens and obsessions also frees attention. The point is that adding projects without allocating sufficient attention, as well as time–energy–money, means program quality and effectiveness will suffer.

5. Strengthening the Culture of Thanksgiving and Celebration

Above, I wrote about the virtue of thankfulness. Virtues are strengthened through their being practiced. Kegan and Lahey write that they often observe clients working in organizations where saying thanks is rare and ineffectively said at that. Each worker gets caught up in the massive amount of work expected. From silo to silo, little thanks are said. Kegan and Lahey argue also that a culture of celebration and saying thanks is essential in tough times. A marriage therapist asserts that couples need to build a positive emotional bank that they draw on when difficulties arise. The same is true in organizations. Kegan and Lahey recommend that leaders regularly build in opportunities to say thanks. They also argue that we should thank the person directly, specifying what we are thankful for, and we should say it in a "non-attributive" way—meaning that we name our experience ("I appreciated the laugh I got out of the joke you told to loosen everyone up") rather than attribute a quality to someone ("You were really funny").[19]

The church should need no outside help in reminding us to celebrate and to say thanks! Check a concordance for how often the Psalms or Paul says thanks and calls us to celebrate. But, especially in times when congregations feel under siege, at odds with an ecology that members perceive to be toxic, it is hard to take the time to say thanks and to throw excellent parties. And, it is precisely at such times that we should strive to weave a congregational culture in which thanksgiving is prominent.

6. Handling Conflict Well

Despite almost two thousand years of practice, most Christian congregations seem ill-prepared to deal with conflict well. Considering that congregations generally have an underdeveloped theological understanding of conflict and demonstrate low emotional intelligence all too frequently, if I were a betting man, I would say the odds are that negotiating the transition from a Christendom congregation to a cruciform congregation will be a battle. There are reasons for and interests invested in macerated clergy and congregations. Moving in directions that challenge those reasons and interests will evoke conflict.

For example, if we agree that theology and spiritual practices matter, but we do not currently spend much time doing either, then—to use Kegan and Lahey again—we might ask, "Which activities do we engage in that leave us without the time, energy, money, attention to invest in theological and spiritual practices? What are the counter-commitment these practices represent? If we stopped those activities, what is your assumption about what would happen?"

This example points toward the primary concept I want to underline regarding conflict: conflicted situations, other than pathological ones in which an endangered person or community must be protected, are tremendous opportunities to learn. In conflict we can come to understand what something means to us. In being confronted with beliefs or values or styles or practices that are different from our own, we can both learn that there is another way and what it is that we hold most dear. We learn to be a community in celebrations, in times of distress, and in the midst of conflict.

Christian communities fundamentally need to learn to learn from conflict. This has always been true. But, given that the speed of change in our time is often overwhelming, that change and conflict are twins, and that we are also participating in a glacial movement from Christendom to a missionary setting in the United States, learning from conflict is essential for us to live well.

Conclusion

The scriptures say that "We love because God first loved us" (1 John 4:19). We might also say that we can pay attention with presence and love because God pays attention to us with presence and love. Both the scriptures and the centuries of the church's experience testify to God's attentive presence with us—along with God's call to us to join in the mission of tending to creation and mending a broken world, in the name of Jesus Christ.

What would your congregation look like if it were a truly attentive congregation, if being present to God and to neighbor "consumed" its life—if you engaged in focal practices that strengthened your ability to pay attention to what God is doing in the world and to join with Christ in that work? What would your congregation look like if worship were the center of the congregation's life and, for the most part, each person gave to worship the attention it deserves? What if you became well known in the community as the congregation where people learned to converse and conflict with one another—as Christians? What if you had so many members practicing detachment or relinquishment that you had a record number of people tithing and giving to the poor from their substance? What if several times each year, especially during the feast seasons of Christmas and Easter, each family contributed their very best foods to share with one another? What if an attitude of thanksgiving permeated your life together and complaints were seldom heard? What if, in the yearly evaluation of the congregation's ministry, you could point to concrete signs that the congregation behaved less anxiously and—better yet—more centered on the reign of God than anyone could remember?

Our attention is the most precious gift we can offer to another. Receiving loving attention is a profoundly rare gift. In this distracting and dissipating age, giving this rare gift wisely and, as Christians, faithfully, will require our attention. The work is hard, as any deep change work is. But the Christian tradition provides us dozens of practices of attending to God and neighbor. If we reach into that tradition, we will find insight into how Jesus attended and clues regarding how the church should attend to the reign of God today.

Notes

Introduction

1. Elevating Mary's choice does not devalue "women's work" or the activity of hospitality per se. Rather, Jesus' action broadens women's role to include learning and being conversation partners with men.

2. It is difficult to know how to label congregations that belong to denominations that we once called mainline. These denominations have been so shifted in the map of U.S. religious life over the last forty years that it is difficult to name them in a way that connotes centrality. Throughout this book, when I use the word *church* or *congregation*, I am speaking primarily of and to these formerly mainline denominations.

3. John J. Ratey, *A User's Guide to the Brain: Perception, Attention, and the Four Theaters of the Brain* (New York: Pantheon, 2001), 117.

4. Thomas H. Davenport and John C. Beck, *The Attention Economy: Understanding the New Currency of Business* (Boston: Harvard Business School Press, 2001); Stephen Bertman, *Hyperculture: The Human Cost of Speed* (Westport, Conn.: Praeger, 1998).

5. Joseph R. Dominguez and Vicki Robin, *Your Money or Your Life: Transforming Your Relationship with Money and Achieving Financial Independence* (New York: Penguin Books, 1999). The authors argue that we underestimate the real cost of our jobs when we fail to take into account all of the self-soothing we buy (such as weekend getaways) in order to cope with the pressure and unsatisfying exchange of paying out our life-energy for money.

6. Web site: http://www.voiceoftheinjured.com/a-aa-cell-phones-accidents-injuries.html. "The popularity of phone-based personal digital assistants and Internet-enabled cell phones may only add to the problem. Will busy workers be able to resist the temptation to conduct a quick Web search during a monotonous morning commute? . . . And, who knows what websites will be browsed. Just how many other things can a driver do while operating a motor vehicle?" This article also cites a 1997 *New England Journal of Medicine* study that claimed

cell phone users are four times as likely to be involved in a traffic accident while using the phone than non-using drivers.

7. Neil Postman, *Amusing Ourselves to Death: Public Discourse in the Age of Show Business* (New York: Penguin, 1986); Mihaly Csikszentmihalyi, *The Evolving Self: A Psychology for the New Millennium* (New York: HarperCollins, 1993); Robert Putnam, *Bowling Alone: The Collapse and Revival of American Community* (New York: Simon & Schuster, 2000).

8. *Oxford English Dictionary*, 2nd ed., 1989 (on-line edition).

9. Note the triple entendre there—to fix as in repair and to fix as in being glued to it; a third meaning, as in fixate, can refer to arrested development, attached to an object that prevents one from growing toward maturity.

10. *Oxford English Dictionary*, 2nd ed., 1989 (on-line edition).

Chapter 1

1. See Mark Chaves, *Congregations in America* (Boston: Harvard University Press, 2004).

2. Christian A. Schwartz, *Natural Church Development: A Guide to Eight Essential Qualities of Healthy Churches* (St. Charles, Ill.: Smart Church Resources, 1996); Rick Warren, *The Purpose-Driven Church: Growth without Compromising Your Message and Mission* (Grand Rapids, Mich.: Zondervan, 1995).

3. Douglas John Hall, *Thinking the Faith: Christian Theology in a North American Context* (Minneapolis: Fortress Press, 1991), 264–65, writes of tradition as a sort of storehouse from which the church can both bring out practices for use and store them away, perhaps to be used another day.

4. See Alasdair C. MacIntyre, *After Virtue: A Study in Moral Theory* (Notre Dame, Ind.: University of Notre Dame Press, 1981); David Tracy, *Plurality and Ambiguity: Hermeneutics, Religion, Hope* (San Francisco: Harper & Row, 1987).

5. See Diana Butler Bass, *The Practicing Congregation: Imagining a New Old Church* (Herndon, Va.: Alban Institute, 2004).

6. See Aaron Spiegel, Nancy Armstrong, and J. Brent Bill, *40 Days and 40 Bytes: Making Computers Work for Your Congregation* (Herndon, Va.: Alban Institute, 2004), which helpfully raises questions about using technology to serve the mission rather than vice versa.

7. Georg Simmel, *Conflict* (London: Collier-Macmillan, 1964).

8. Congregations are like organisms. They live in ecologies that contain resources they need to live, and they must return something positive to the environment in order to keep the environment habitable. When an ecology changes, the organism must adapt, move, or die. An organism receives its environment as toxic when either the nutrients it used to draw disappear or when those nutrients cannot be received without also receiving elements that sap life rather than give it.

9. Paul D. Hanson, *The People Called: The Growth of Community in the Bible* (San Francisco: Harper & Row, 1986).

10. Lewis Seymour Mudge, *The Sense of a People: Toward a Church for the Human Future* (Philadelphia: Trinity Press International, 1992).

11. I will develop this point in chapter 5.

12. Robert Kegan and Lisa Laskow Lahey, *How the Way We Talk Can Change the Way We Work: Seven Languages for Transformation* (San Francisco: Jossey-Bass, 2001).

13. Ronald A. Heifitz, *Leadership without Easy Answers* (Cambridge, Mass.: Belknap Press of Harvard University Press, 1994).

Chapter 2

1. Augustine, *Confessions*, Book IX, ed. Gillian Clark (Cambridge: Cambridge University Press, 1995).

2. Carol Zaleski, "Attending to Attention," in *Faithful Imagining: Essays in Honor of Richard R. Niebuhr*, ed. Sang Hyun Lee, Wayne Proudfoot, and Albert L. Blackwell, Scholars Press Homage Series 19 (Atlanta: Scholars Press, 1995), 128.

3. In Genesis 30:25-43, we have the story of Jacob breeding sheep in front of "striped, speckled, and spotted" rods in order to produce an offspring with similar markings. There is also a fascinating scholarly debate regarding understandings of the relationship between light and the eye in ancient world. Some ancients believed that light emanated from the eye, rather than that the sun was the source of light and the eye a receptor. See Hans Dieter Betz, *The Sermon on the Mount*, Hermeneia, ed. Adela Yarbro Collins (Minneapolis: Fortress Press, 1995), 439–53.

4. William James, *The Principles of Psychology*, vol. 1 (New York: Dover, 1950 [1890]), 403–04.

5. Jorge Luis Borges, "Funes the Memorious," in *Ficciones*, trans. Anthony Kerrigan (1962), ed. John Sturrock (New York: Alfred A. Knopf/Everyman, 1993 [1942]), 83–91. Available from http://www.bridgewater.edu/~atrupe/GEC101/Funes.html; accessed May 28, 2003.

6. See Harold E. Pashler, *The Psychology of Attention* (Cambridge, Mass.: The MIT Press, 1998), esp. chap. 5, 217–61.

7. John J. Ratey, *A User's Guide to the Brain: Perception, Attention, and the Four Theaters of the Brain* (New York: Vintage Books, 2002), 3–13, 110–29.

8. For scientific backup for my viewpoint, I encourage you to read brain researcher Jeffrey Schwartz, with Sharon Begley, *The Mind and the Brain: Neuroplasticity and the Power of Mental Force* (New York: ReganBooks/HarperCollins, 2002). Dr. Schwartz has written a fascinating account of how teaching persons with obsessive-compulsive disorder to refocus their attention

when tempted to engage their dysfunctional behaviors has helped them immensely and has even changed brain activity.

9. A book that is an excellent expression of Western cognitive psychology and Buddhist psychology and practice is Tara Bennett-Goleman, *Emotional Alchemy: How the Mind Can Heal the Heart* (New York: Three Rivers Press, 2001).

10. Daniel Goleman, *Destructive Emotions: How Can We Overcome Them? A Scientific Dialogue with the Dalai Lama* (New York: Bantam Books, 2004).

11. The texts, entitled the *Philokalia*, are available inexpensively through used-book suppliers, in the four-volume paperback edition translated and edited by G. E. H. Palmer, Philip Sherrard, and Kallistos Ware (London: Faber & Faber, 1983–1999).

12. John Wesley, "On Dissipation," from *Wesley's Sermons*, 1872 ed., Christian Classics Ethereal Library. Available from http://www.ccel.org/ccel/wesley/sermons.vi.xxvi.html#vi.xxvi-p0.2; accessed Aug. 17, 2004.

13. Simone Weil, *Waiting for God*, trans. Emma Craufurd (New York: Perennial, 2001), 62.

14. Ibid., 64.

15. Ibid., 65.

16. Ibid., 64.

17. http://www.adage.com/news.cms?newsId=40256; accessed May 18, 2004.

18. Thomas H. Davenport and John C. Beck, *The Attention Economy: Understanding the New Currency of Business* (Boston: Harvard Business School Press, 2001), 20–21.

19. Ibid., 27.

20. Neil Postman, *Amusing Ourselves to Death: Public Discourse in the Age of Show Business* (New York: Penguin Books, 1986).

Chapter 3

1. Bernard Brandon Scott, *Hear Then the Parable: A Commentary on the Parables of Jesus* (Minneapolis: Fortress Press, 1989), 8.

2. Ibid., 39.

3. Ibid., 56, 61–62.

4. Contrary to the way individual Christians tend to read the Bible, biblical scholars teach that the Bible's primary audience is the assembled congregation, rather than individuals per se.

5. Scott, *Hear Then the Parable*, 61.

6. I am indebted to Scott's discussion of these parables. See ibid., esp. 321–87.

7. Henri J. M. Nouwen, *Reaching Out: The Three Movements of the Spiritual Life* (Garden City, N.Y.: Doubleday, 1975).

8. Many scholars pick up the teaching on anxiety at v. 25 because they believe that Matthew, as editor of Jesus' stories and sayings, decided to situate this section of Jesus' teaching within the frame here. Consequently, the "therefore" that opens v. 25 may not originally have referred to the teachings on treasure, the eye, and serving only one master. But whether the "do not be anxious" discussion sits in its original setting or not, the way we have it is the way it has come down through the centuries and has provided powerful practical wisdom for the church.

9. This is the central insight of Joseph R. Dominguez and Vicki Robin, *Your Money or Your Life: Transforming Your Relationship with Money and Achieving Financial Independence* (New York: Penguin Books, 1999).

10. See Hans Dieter Betz, *The Sermon on the Mount*, Hermeneia, ed. Adela Yarbro Collins (Minneapolis: Fortress Press, 1995), 437–53, for a discussion of the eye as lamp and whether the ancients thought of the eye as a source of light per se or an expression of the person's inner moral light.

11. Robert K. Greenleaf and Larry C. Spears, *Servant Leadership: A Journey into the Nature of Legitimate Power and Greatness* (New York: Paulist Press, 2002).

12. John Wesley, "Upon Our Lord's Sermon on the Mount (IX)," 29 (1872 edition), available at http://gbgm-umc.org/umhistory/wesley/sermons/serm-029.stm; accessed February 24, 2005.

13. Betz, *Sermon on the Mount*, 461–64.

14. Betz writes that anxiety is not a concept in the Hebrew Bible per se but shows up in the Greek version, especially wisdom texts. Other New Testament texts on anxiety include Mark 4:19 and its parallels; Matt. 10:19; Luke 10:41, 21:34; 1 Cor. 7:32-34, 12:25; 2 Cor .11:28; Phil. 2:20, 4:6; 1 Pet. 5:7. See Ibid., 463 n. 324.

15. http://www.ccel.org/a/aquinas/catena/Matthew/ch06.htm; accessed July 5, 2004.

16. http://www.episcopalian.org/austin/lectionary/trinity15/LutherGospel.htm; accessed February 25, 2005.

17. Wesley, "Upon Our Lord's Sermon on the Mount (IX)," 29.

18. Dietrich Bonhoeffer, *The Cost of Discipleship*, trans. R. H. Fuller (London: SCM Press, 1951), 201.

19. Albert Schweitzer and John Bowden, *The Quest for the Historical Jesus: The First Complete Edition*, Fortress Classics in Biblical Studies (Minneapolis: Fortress Press, 2001).

Chapter Four

1. Robert Wuthnow makes this point in *After Heaven: Spirituality in America since the 1950s* (Berkeley: University of California Press, 1998).

2. Douglas John Hall, *The Cross in Our Context: Jesus and the Suffering World* (Minneapolis: Fortress Press, 2003), 3.

3. I imply no judgment on those persons and couples who must work an ungodly number of hours in the wage economy at minimum wage. But patterns for U.S. workers with better salaries are very interesting when compared with Europeans; U.S. workers shop much more and vacation less than our European counterparts. See Joanne B. Ciulla, *The Working Life: The Promise and Betrayal of Modern Work* (New York: Crown Business, 2000), 200.

4. Joseph R. Dominguez and Vicki Robin, *Your Money or Your Life: Transforming Your Relationship with Money and Achieving Financial Independence* (New York: Penguin Books, 1999).

5. Margaret Visser, *The Rituals of Dinner: The Origins, Evolution, Eccentricities, and Meaning of Table Manners* (New York: Grove Weidenfeld, 1991).

6. To cite just a few of the very good books on conflict in congregations: David W. Augsburger, *Conflict Mediation across Cultures: Pathways and Patterns* (Louisville: Westminster John Knox, 1992); Charles H. Cosgrove and Dennis D. Hatfield, *Church Conflict: The Hidden Systems Behind the Fights* (Nashville: Abingdon, 1994); Hugh F. Halverstadt, *Managing Church Conflict* (Louisville: Westminster John Knox, 1991); Peter L. Steinke, *Healthy Congregations: A Systems Approach* (Bethesda, Md.: Alban Institute, 1996); Wayne E. Oates, *The Care of Troublesome People* (Bethesda, Md.: Alban Institute, 1994); Speed Leas, *Discover Your Conflict Management Style*, revised ed. (Bethesda, Md.: Alban Institute, 1997); David B. Lott, ed., *Conflict Management in Congregations* (Bethesda, Md.: Alban Institute, 2001).

7. For a polished, profound version of this practice, see the renowned Old Testament scholar Walter Brueggemann's *Awed to Heaven, Rooted in Earth: Prayers of Walter Brueggemann,* ed. Edwin Searcy (Minneapolis: Fortress Press, 2003).

A Theological Conversation

1. Numerous authors in recent years have written about the transition in North America from a "Christian culture" understanding to the viewpoint that North America is a mission opportunity. One well-known book is Loren B. Mead's *The Once and Future Church: Reinventing the Congregation for a New Mission Frontier* (Bethesda, Md.: Alban Institute, 1991). There is a Gospel and Our Culture Network that promotes this missional point of view; see, for example, Darrell L. Guder and Lois Barrett, *Missional Church: A Vision for the Sending of the Church in North America,* Gospel and Our Culture Series (Grand Rapids, Mich.: Wm. B. Eerdmans, 1998).

2. Rick Warren, *The Purpose-Driven Church: Growth without Compromising Your Mission and Your Message* (Grand Rapids, Mich.: Zondervan, 1995); Letty M. Russell, *Church in the Round: Feminist Interpretation of the Church* (Louisville: Westminster John Knox, 1993); Carlyle Fielding Stewart, *The Empowerment Church: Speaking a New Language for Church Growth* (Nashville: Abingdon, 2001); Douglas John Hall, *The Cross in Our Context: Jesus and the Suffering World* (Minneapolis: Fortress Press, 2003).

3. Warren, *Purpose-Driven Church*, 268.

4. Ibid., 63.

5. Russell, *Church in the Round*, 113.

6. Henri J. M. Nouwen, *Reaching Out: The Three Movements of the Spiritual Life* (Garden City, N.Y.: Doubleday, 1975).

7. Stewart, *The Empowerment Church*, 17.

8. Hall, *The Cross in Our Context*, 55, 152.

9. Ibid., 8.

10. Ibid., 6. Hall quotes German theologian Jürgen Moltmann, saying that the theology of the cross tradition has been '"never much loved."'

Chapter 5

1. Dorothy C. Bass, ed., *Practicing Our Faith: A Way of Life for a Searching People* (San Francisco: Jossey-Bass, 1997). This book contains essays on different practices; some of the essays have been expanded into books. See Bass's *Receiving the Day: Christian Practices for Opening the Gift of Time*, The Practices of Faith Series (San Francisco: Jossey-Bass Publishers, 2000); Bass and Don C. Richter, *Way to Live: Christian Practices for Teens* (Nashville: Upper Room Books, 2002); and Stephanie Paulsell, *Honoring the Body: Meditations on a Christian Practice*, The Practices of Faith Series (San Francisco: Jossey-Bass, 2002). A few other books on practices include Thomas G. Long, *Testimony: Talking Ourselves into Being Christian* (San Francisco: Jossey-Bass, 2004); Martha Ellen Stortz, *A World According to God: Practices for Putting Faith at the Center of Your Life* (San Francisco: Jossey-Bass, 2004); Diana Butler Bass, *The Practicing Congregation: Imagining a New Old Church* (Herndon, Va.: Alban Institute, 2004); Gil Rendle and Alice Mann, *Holy Conversations: Strategic Planning as a Spiritual Practice for Congregations* (Bethesda, Md.: Alban Institute, 2003).

2. Loren B. Mead, *The Once and Future Church: Reinventing the Congregation for a New Mission Frontier* (Washington, D.C.: Alban Institute, 1991).

3. http://www.scouting.org/nav/enter.jsp?s=mc&c=mv; accessed Dec. 13, 2004.

4. Albert Borgmann, *Technology and the Character of Contemporary Life: A Philosophical Inquiry* (Chicago: University of Chicago Press, 1984), 4.

5. Ibid., 41ff.

6. Jeffrey M. Schwartz, with Sharon Begley, *The Mind and the Brain: Neuroplasticity and the Power of Mental Force* (New York: ReganBooks/ HarperCollins, 2002). On p. 212, Schwartz writes about an experiment with monkeys. In the experiment, stimulation alone did not remap the monkey's cortices; "it is the attention that counts."

7. Ellen J. Langer, *Mindfulness* (Cambridge, Mass.: Perseus Books, 1989); *The Power of Mindful Learning* (Cambridge, Mass.: Perseus Books, 1997).

8. In addition to the books on practices cited above, one might consult: Mark Lau Branson, *Memories, Hopes, and Conversations: Appreciative Inquiry and Congregational Change* (Herndon, Va.: Alban Institute, 2004); Thomas G. Long, *Beyond the Worship Wars: Building Vital and Faithful Worship* (Bethesda, Md.: Alban Institute, 2001); Michael Durall, *Creating Congregations of Generous People* (Bethesda, Md.: Alban Institute, 1999); Craig R. Dykstra, *Growing in the Life of Faith: Education and Christian Practices* (Louisville: Geneva Press, 1999); Stephen H. Webb, *Good Eating*, Christian Practice of Everyday Life Series (Grand Rapids, Mich.: Brazos Press, 2001).

9. Paul D. Hanson, *The People Called: The Growth of Community in the Bible* (San Francisco: Harper & Row, 1986).

10. Annie Dillard, *Teaching a Stone to Talk: Expeditions and Encounters* (New York: Harper & Row, 1982), 40–41.

11. David Tracy, *Plurality and Ambiguity: Hermeneutics, Religion, and Hope* (San Francisco: Harper & Row, 1987), ix.

12. A list of best practices for conversation in ecumenical circles is found in Robert McAfee Brown's *The Ecumenical Revolution: An Interpretation of the Catholic–Protestant Dialogue* (London: Burns & Oates, 1969).

13. The United Methodist Church, *The United Methodist Hymnal* (Nashville: United Methodist Publishing House, 1989), #178.

14. Joanne B. Ciulla, *The Working Life: The Promise and Betrayal of Modern Work* (New York: Crown Business, 2000); Joseph R. Dominguez and Vicki Robin, *Your Money or Your Life: Transforming Your Relationship with Money and Achieving Financial Independence* (New York: Penguin Books, 1999).

Chapter 6

1. Joseph Sittler, "The Maceration of the Minister," available online at http://www.religion-online.org/showchapter.asp?title=795&C=975; accessed Jan. 30, 2004, emphasis mine.

2. H. Richard Niebuhr, *The Kingdom of God in America* (Middletown, Ct.: Wesleyan University Press, 1988 [1937]), 193.

3. Dietrich Bonhoeffer, *The Cost of Discipleship* (New York: Macmillan, 1963; [1937]); *Letters and Papers from Prison* (New York: Macmillan, 1972).

4. Daniel Goleman, *Emotional Intelligence* (New York: Bantam Books, 1995).

5. Ronald A. Heifetz, *Leadership without Easy Answers* (Cambridge, Mass.: Belknap Press of Harvard University Press, 1994).

6. The Serenity Prayer, available from http://www.addictions.org/ serenity.htm#SELFprayer; accessed Nov. 9, 2003. The Twelve Steps, Alcoholics Anonymous, available from http://www.alcoholics-anonymous.org/default/ en_about_aa_sub.cfm?subpageid=17&pageid=24; accessed Nov. 9, 2003.

7. The slow food movement's Web site is http://www.slowfood.com.

8. Ellen J. Langer, *Mindfulness* (Cambridge, Mass.: Perseus Books, 1989); *The Power of Mindful Learning* (Cambridge, Mass.: Perseus Books, 1998).

9. For example, recently I heard two different approaches to a stewardship campaign demonstrated in the same Sunday service. The campaign chair spoke about the gap between the projected budget and this year's giving. Contrary to all current literature on stewardship and on why people give, he focused on funding the budget and tried to motivate people to give more by asking them to consider the "return on their investment." In contrast, the pastor's sermon on the widow's mite challenged people to give from their substance because God has created us to give. In order to be human, we must give of our lives, a portion of which is represented in our financial stewardship.

10. Douglas John Hall, *Thinking the Faith: Christian Theology in a North American Context* (Minneapolis: Fortress Press, 1991), 19.

11. There are significant exceptions to this statement, notably those authors who urge Christians to seek the lost *and* to share in their suffering; e.g., Thomas G. Bandy, *Moving Off the Map: A Field Guide to Changing the Congregation* (Nashville: Abingdon, 1998), 38.

12. Robert Kegan and Lisa Laskow Lahey, *How the Way We Talk Can Change the Way We Work: Seven Languages for Transformation* (San Francisco: Jossey-Bass, 2001).

13. Ibid., 21–88.

14. Thomas H. Davenport and John C. Beck, *The Attention Economy: Understanding the New Currency of Business* (Boston: Harvard Business School Press, 2001).

15. Jim Loehr and Tony Schwartz, *The Power of Full Engagement* (New York: Simon & Schuster, 2003).

16. I recommend several resources. First, Tara Bennett Goleman, *Emotional Alchemy: How the Mind Can Heal the Heart* (New York: Three Rivers Press, 2001). Goleman is a therapist who works with a combination of cognitive psychology, emotional intelligence, and Buddhist meditative practice. This book

could be an excellent small-group study. A classic Christian meditation primer is St. Ignatius's spiritual exercises, available in many editions. Another book is Ken McLeod's *Waking Up to Your Life: Discovering the Buddhist Path of Attention* (San Francisco: HarperSanFrancisco, 2001). This is a serious book, not for the faint-hearted. The meditations he suggests from Buddhist tradition have some affinity with St. Ignatius's spiritual exercises, for both involve facing impermanence, disease, and death. I also recommend checking out the Web site http://www.mindandlife.org, which describes a research project designed to test the effect of meditation on people's ability to practice emotional intelligence. The multidisciplinary project grew out of a long collaboration between Western scientists, philosophers, and the Dalai Lama. It is a project and a conversation in which the church ought to have a profound stake.

17. Bob Sitze, *Not Trying Too Hard: New Basics for Sustainable Congregations* (Bethesda, Md.: Alban Institute, 2001); see esp. pp. 107–12.

18. Kegan and Lahey, *The Way We Talk*, 63.

19. Ibid., 91–102. The marital therapist is John Gottman. See John M. Gottman and Nan Silver, *The Seven Principles for Making Marriage Work: A Practical Guide from the Country's Foremost Relationship Expert* (New York: Three Rivers Press, 1999).

"Gary Peluso-Verdend is determined to get congregations less obsessed with novelty as their chief goal and efficiency as their governing principle and more finely tuned to delivering meaning and purpose that celebrates God in their midst."

–Peter W. Marty, from the foreword

paying attention

"'Attention is the origin of faith, hope, and love,' according to Nicephorus the Solitary, a fourteenth-century monk of Mt. Athos, and many Christian writers agree: the way we attend or fail to attend to God and neighbor is a real measure of our spiritual life. Now Gary Peluso-Verdend applies this principle to the lives of congregations, offering a practical, hopeful, lucid, and graceful guide to the flourishing of congregations in an epoch of ever-increasing distraction."

–Carol Zaleski, Smith College

"This is much-needed advice in a world filled with books on 40 days to a better church, programs in a box, and easy steps to Christian community. *Paying Attention* leads us into the deep places of the soul—the places where congregations pay attention to the unique mission to which God has called them."

–J. Brent Bill, author of *Holy Silence: The Gift of Quaker Spirituality*

Gary Peluso-Verdend, a native of the Chicago area, is vice president for institutional advancement at Phillips Theological Seminary in Tulsa, Oklahoma. He is an ordained minister in the United Methodist Church and has served on the pastoral staff of several congregations.

ISBN 1-56699-308-3

9 781566 993081

90000

THE
ALBAN
INSTITUTE
www.alban.org